Careers
Without Reschooling

CAREERS
WITHOUT
RESCHOOLING

The Survival Guide
to the Job Hunt
for Liberal Arts Graduates

◆ ◆ ◆

DICK GOLDBERG

Edited by Katharine Kazan

CONTINUUM • NEW YORK

1986
The Continuum Publishing Company
370 Lexington Avenue, New York, N.Y. 10017

Printed in the United States of America

Library of Congress Cataloging in Publication Data
Goldberg, Dick, 1943-
Careers without reschooling.

1. Job hunting—United States.   2. College graduates—
Employment—United States.   I. Title.
HF5382.75.U6G65 1985   650.1'4   85-5926
ISBN 0-8264-0355-7 (pbk.)

Contents

Acknowledgments   viii

Introduction
The Special Case of the Liberal Arts Graduate   1

PART ONE: THE JOB HUNT

Chapter 1: Career Insights for the Liberal Arts Graduate   5
RICHARD NELSON BOLLES

*"Nobody is better prepared to go about the job hunt
than the liberal arts graduate."*

Chapter 2: Look Inside Yourself   19
MAY FRAYDAS

*"It's no small thing to convince a college graduate
that he or she really does have marketable skills."*

Chapter 3: Make Your Resumé Work for You   29
KIRBY STANAT

*"Take your resumé and hand it to a friend, and ask them,
'Do you understand what I just said in that resumé?'"*

Chapter 4: The Hidden Job Market   37
MARY KAUPFER & TOM JOHNSON

*"The biggest problem for humanities graduates is not
the employer. Their biggest problem is themselves."*

Chapter 5: How to Make the Interviewer Want You   45
KIRBY STANAT

"Both of us should realize that we're on a blind date."

Chapter 6: Special Issues of the Returning Homemaker   55
LISA MUNRO & SAMANTHA RIVER

"Maturity is one thing that a homemaker can always sell."

Chapter 7: Successful Career Switching   69
LESLIE GOLDSMITH & CYNTHIA KABAT

*"What's wrong with me? Why can't I stay with this?
I prepared for this: I should like it."*

PART TWO : INFORMATIONAL INTERVIEWS

Chapter 8: Advertising Account Executive   85

*"You hear that a number of people in the advertising business
are workaholics. It's not so much that they want to be;
it's that they have to be."*

Chapter 9: Public Relations Specialist   97

*"I have a tourism client, I have a medical client,
and I have a pizza client. I have to understand
all these different businesses."*

Chapter 10: Advertising Copywriter   107

*"You have to love words, love to play with them and
make them effective . . . you have to want to have fun."*

Chapter 11: Editor   117

"Good judgement is the first and foremost thing."

Chapter 12: Helping Professional   127

*"If you love your client like you love your brother,
you sometimes find yourself in trouble."*

Chapter 13: New Police Officer   137

"There's a real closeness, a comraderie here on the police force. I didn't find that when I was in education."

Chapter 14: Life Insurance Agent   147

"We find that a lot of the problem with image is in the agents' own minds."

Chapter 15: Stockbroker   157

"If I market anything, I probably market myself."

Chapter 16: Fund Raiser   167

"I love the challenge and the puzzle of trying to collect resources where there weren't any before."

Chapter 17: Small Business Owner   177

"If you want to be the King of Pizza, you better know pizza before you start selling it."

Chapter 18: Retail Manager   187

"I teach every day. Retail has a high turnover and I have new people every day coming to me for training."

Chapter 19: TV and Radio Producer   197

"The primary criteria for being a public television producer are that you have to be a generalist and you have to have a lust for learning."

Chapter 20: Real Estate Agent   207

"I think of everything this business has to offer, the thing I value most is the independence."

Chapter 21: Now What?   217

"What if none of these fourteen careers grabs you? Here are 176 other possibilities."

Acknowledgments

First and foremost, I owe my gratitude to Katie Kazan, who not only transcribed and edited the tapes of the interviews but also was largely responsible for hatching the idea of making this book from an audio-cassette album. She is a highly skilled craftswoman and was a delight to work with on this project. Thanks also to Beth Miller for her professionalism and for going that extra mile in producing the audio-cassette album upon which this book is based, and to Faye Alroy who so ably edited the original tape interviews to their final, more listenable versions. My thanks also to public radio station WHA and to its manager, Jack Mitchell, for their cooperation and assistance in taping these interviews.

Finally, to the forty people who shared so much valuable information, as well as parts of themselves, a deep thanks for providing the core fuel for this project.

Introduction
THE SPECIAL CASE OF
THE LIBERAL ARTS GRADUATE

Over the last seven years, I've produced and hosted hundreds of talk shows for public radio and television. Almost all have dealt with my two consuming interests, business and psychology, and perhaps fifty have directly addressed the issues of careers and the job hunt. In these discussions, the interrelationship of business and psychology is most direct, and the same issues are raised time and again. Why does one individual succeed in a particular business while another, equally talented, fails? What are the psychological components of success? To what extent can attitudes be defeating and self-knowledge enabling? Just how important is enjoyment to a successful career?

The most interesting people I interview, on any subject at all, have in common the fact that they've survived a struggle, a rite of passage. This is the struggle of, "Who am I and why does the world need me?" Its survivors include managers, sales people, and counselors; nationally acclaimed public figures and local business people for whom privacy is of premium importance. These are people who have gotten off the track, who have suffered a bit and thought about the world and how they might fit in. They are not the rule followers, but rather the people who ask, "Why?" and perhaps more often, "Why not?"

Liberal arts graduates have the good fortune to be able to face this struggle. Their education will have given them a foundation of general and specific skills and information, it will have taught them to analyze and self-examine, but it will *not* have given them a title by which to identify themselves and their career options. For many a liberal arts graduate, this is a frustrating situation: if they cannot plug right into a job, what was the point of all that effort and expense? If they are not nurses or computer scientists or lab technicians, the world doesn't seem to know what to do with them.

They must decide what to do with themselves.

The liberal arts graduate has the unfair and inappropriate reputation of being unemployable. That reputation is dead wrong. As you'll learn throughout this book, people are employed for who they are and what they can do, not because of a label of competence. The very qualities nurtured by a liberal arts education are the qualities that can lead to a successful job hunt and career; the problem is that often the liberal arts graduate doesn't realize that he or she has these skills. The interviews in this book will prove very reassuring on that score.

The first seven interviews are with career guidance experts, men and women who advise others professionally as they search for employment. The thirteen informational interviews that follow are with liberal arts graduates who have found careers that are fulfilling and diverse. They discuss how they entered these fields, the day-to-day pleasures and frustrations of their work, their salaries, and what the future is likely to hold for them.

This book may create one large problem for you: it puts the ball in your court. After reading it, you'll see that you do have the tools, you do have the abilities, and you do have the way. You need only ask yourself if you have the will.

Good luck,
Dick Goldberg

PART ONE

◆ ◆ ◆

The Job Hunt

CHAPTER 1

Career Insights for the Liberal Arts Graduate

Nobody is better prepared to go about the job hunt than the liberal arts graduate. The skills it takes to do the job hunt are the very skills the liberal arts graduate has been working on for four years in college.

—Richard Nelson Bolles

RICHARD NELSON BOLLES, through his book *What Color Is Your Parachute?*, has offered reassurance and direction to a generation of job hunters. First published in 1970, *Parachute* has been imitated in style and content, but it remains the best-selling career guidance book on the market today. Bolles's other books are *The Three Boxes of Life and How to Get Out of Them* and, with John Crystal, *Where Do I Go from Here with My Life?* He is the director of the National Career Development Project in Walnut Creek, California.

We begin this chapter with a description of some of the theories through which Bolles has revolutionized job hunting in this country. From there we explore examples of how these theories might apply to actual situations, and how the liberal arts graduate, through both the specific skills and the broad concepts learned in college, has a distinct advantage in the search for a satisfying career.

GOLDBERG: Would you describe some of the basic premises and philosophies that distinguish you from others in the career search field?

BOLLES: One concept I stress is that career change and job hunting are repetitive activities for every working person in this country today. According to present statistics, the average job in America, at least when people are new to the job market, lasts something like 3.6 years. The average person will have ten employers in his or her lifetime and three distinct careers.

Considering these statistics, my concept is really a commonsense conclusion. I say that when you're looking for a job, it's not enough to merely find the job. You must also learn how to conduct the search, for you are surely going to have to do it again. And any time people help us with the job search, the mark of their helpfulness is the degree to which they empower us for the rest of our lives by teaching us the skills and realities of the search.

This is particularly true of colleges. It isn't sufficient to say, "We help every graduate find a job," because that implies that the only time graduates are ever going to go job hunting is the minute they get out of college. A much more valid claim would be, "We help teach every student who graduates from this institution how to go about job hunting for the rest of their lives."

Another idea that is distinctive, or at least was when I first published *Parachute* in 1970, is that all job-hunting and career-changing strategies can break down into two "families" of ideas, or processes.

The first family has been tagged "the numbers game," and it's comparable to going to Las Vegas and playing as many one-armed bandits as you can, on the theory that eventually one of them will pay off for you. Essentially, it says if you try this strategy and that strategy and all these other strategies, one of them will probably land you a job. But none of them by themselves, no *one* job-hunting method actually works very well.

GOLDBERG: How do the number of job openings compare to the number of applicants for any one job?

BOLLES: A study published some years ago surveyed jobs offered by a considerable number of companies. When you sifted through the statistics that were in that study, it turned out one job was offered for every 1,470 resumés that went out. So from the employer's point of view, 1,469 people had to pass under his or her nose before finally finding somebody to link up with a vacancy.

The numbers game is a search for vacancies, but the other family of job-hunting strategies, which I advocate, argues that you ought not to go after vacancies. Instead, it suggests that you look at anyplace that intrigues you, where you might like to work, and approach it whether or not you know a vacancy exists.

In the numbers game, the theory is that you're at the mercy of the forces of the marketplace. In this alternate family of strategies, which I call "creative job hunting," the assumption is that the job hunter has a lot more power to create what is occurring in the job market than he or she might first suppose. Our economy leaps by an enormous number of jobs every year, and in part, the strategies of the job hunter help to create those jobs.

GOLDBERG: Would you give us an example?

BOLLES: Suppose you're thinking of hiring an assistant, but you're so involved with your broadcasts that you're not doing anything about it. Then suddenly you're approached by somebody who's taking more initiative than the average job hunter. You might well say, "This is just the kind of person I'm looking for!"

So that person doesn't plant the idea of a job in your head, but he or she certainly galvanizes all the forces that are moving toward creating a new job.

GOLDBERG: Can you guess how the number of advertised job openings compares to those available in the informal way you just described?

BOLLES: I have no idea, and I don't think anyone else does either. Our country does not keep good enough statistics on anything. As an example, you have only to consider the unemployment figure bandied about every month by the government. They interview people from about 55,000 households a month, and they say, "Tell me what you are doing during the month."

You might say, "I'm job hunting six days a week, but I go down and help my brother Ed with his gas station Monday nights. He needs a little extra help and he pays me a few bucks, but otherwise I'm still looking."

Immediately the government takes you off the unemployment rolls. If you work one hour for anybody during the month, you are no longer unemployed in their view. And thus do they structure the figure to be the lowest that they can get it, because the number of unemployed in the country is always political dynamite regardless of which party happens to be in power.

GOLDBERG: That's bad news, then. Unemployment is really worse than it seems.

BOLLES: That's right.

GOLDBERG: But I'm confused. You've said that there are a lot more jobs out there than the numbers indicate, but on the other hand you're saying that there's also more unemployment.

BOLLES: There are indeed many more people unemployed than statistics indicate, but there are not that many more people job hunting. There's a big difference.

In our culture, a lot of people, in fact a mind-boggling number of people, are willing to accept what I would call subsistence-level living. Just to speak from my own personal knowledge, two of my friends became unemployed during the past year and a half. They had always had very invigorating kinds of jobs, as far as I understood, and I assumed they would immediately go out and find other jobs. But they were at a point in their lives where they were in a mood to just coast. And so, the fact that there are probably many more unemployed than the government will admit will not necessarily make the situation worse for the job hunter.

GOLDBERG: I've heard you say that you're not the expert, that no one's really the expert. So who knows what? It's all so confusing.

BOLLES: One of the great difficulties in this field of career planning, or life/work planning, is that everybody's hungry for an expert. Everybody wants somebody who will have statistics at his or her fingertips and some kind of a magic box where they can crank in their factors and have it answer, "This is what you should be!" In my view, this search for an expert inhibits people from successful job hunting more than anything else.

GOLDBERG: What do you think of the notion that if you're a liberal arts graduate you need to go back to college or technical school and get a degree to qualify for a certain career?

BOLLES: An assumption is made in our culture that your degree should define your job. The assumption is not only that it should define it when you first get out of college, but that it should still be defining it twenty years later. And increasingly, people are saying, "Baloney!" Even an engineering graduate may say twenty years later, "I don't want to be doing this!"

We let the decisions about what degree to pursue and what job to pursue sound as though they're two parts of the same decision. They're not; they may not be related at all.

The *only thing* that anybody has to know is: "What do I most want to do with my life? Is it possible for me to go out and find that thing, if it already exists, or is it possible for me to go out and create it?"

GOLDBERG: Suppose you decide that you absolutely want to teach third grade in Kenosha, Wisconsin, where there's now a waiting list of six hundred people and a clear, time-based hiring procedure.

BOLLES: There are two important things to remember. First, look very carefully at the hiring process for that kind of job. If the Kenosha public school system really bases its hiring procedure only on a time factor, that would be about the first job I've ever heard of where the hiring process actually functioned the way claimed. There's always a myth about how it works, and then the actual way it works.

Let me give you an example outside of the school system. I know a man who hires for the federal government—positions that require the civil service examination. He told me, "If I interviewed someone and liked him and he was interested in a vacancy that was available at that time, I would indeed have to require him to take the civil service exam. But if you don't think I could figure out a way to get him into that position, then I'm not worth the salary they're paying me."

GOLDBERG: So what you're saying is: Think! You've got to think.

BOLLES: Yes, and you've got to get beyond assuming that you know how things really work in the job market or in the job-hunting process. It takes some intelligent questions to find out how people actually get hired. So that would be my first answer, but only my first, to your example of the third-grade teacher. I would say to your teacher, "Study how people actually get hired there. Try to find somebody who *didn't* get hired by the official procedure and talk to that person."

GOLDBERG: Would that be your advice in any hiring situation?

BOLLES: Yes. But what if your teacher examines the hiring process and it *is* exactly as asserted? That leads to another concept I have talked about for some years, which is that people become transfixed prematurely on a job title.

You might say, "I have skills I call teaching skills that I love to use." I would ask, "But what are these skills?" Some people love to teach drawing and some people love to teach English. Some people love to grade papers, other people hate grading papers. So you can first break down an umbrella term like teaching into its separate components.

Also, if you say, "I like to teach third grade," you are identifying the kind of client or object of your skills that you like. In this case, you are saying, "I don't want to work with adults, I don't want to work with nursery school children, I want to work with third-graders."

So the task becomes one of identifying what other organizations there are in the Kenosha area that work with children of that age and use some of the principal skills that you have called teaching skills. And I would be exceedingly surprised if the answer turned out to be only the Kenosha public school system. That just doesn't happen.

GOLDBERG: Where does the job hunt begin?

BOLLES: It begins with the issue "Why do you want to hunt for a job?" The first motive many people mention is the need for money. You'll hear young people say, "I want a job so that I can have my own place and my own life." For other people, it will start with a desire to be doing something useful and meaningful with their lives. The same person who, at eighteen, would do anything that would bring in money, at the age of forty may be infinitely more particular. The mature person's job hunt, then, will begin with a very different motivation.

Also, there are a number of issues people work on in their lives that spill over into the job hunt. When they're first employed, in their teens, they want to find out what it's like to be in the world of work, what it's like to wait on customers, make change, take orders, and that sort of thing. Next, there's the issue of survival. "Once I have a pretty good idea of what's happening, can I make it? Will I survive?" And beyond that is the issue of mission and meaning. "How do I find something I can commit myself to wholeheartedly?" Those are the people I tend to see.

GOLDBERG: Let me be naive and ask what values have to do with choosing a career.

BOLLES: First, values are crucial in job choice because they determine whether someone likes best to work with data or people or things.

Many people are in jobs where they are dealing primarily with people, when their set of values would rather have them dealing with ideas. All day long they'll feel the pull and say to themselves, "This isn't where I should be." They may have rich skills in dealing with people, but if their real preference is dealing with ideas, that value will make them miserable as long as they have that job.

I'll tell you a story about that. There was a career counselor in Minneapolis who had a friend tell him, "I'm really not very happy with what I'm doing." The counselor knew of a seminar somewhere in Colorado, and he said, "My advice to you is take your money, make the trip, go to the seminar."

When the guy came back, he was ready to kill the career counselor. He'd spent $500 or more going to the seminar and all he'd come out with is that he loved to play bridge. So the counselor said, "What's wrong with that, for heaven's sake? Why don't you try playing bridge on weekends? Why don't you teach it or whatever you want to do with it?"

And the friend said, "Yeah, I'd like to teach bridge. Then I could play it all day." So he taught it on Friday nights and weekends, and to make a long story short, what he did became so popular that he had to abandon his business. He franchised into a number of other cities and ended up making about twice the salary he was making as a businessman when he was doing something he hated.

GOLDBERG: There are workshops for liberal arts graduates and people who've had unfulfilled career aspirations that are based specifically on the premise that you're *not* going to score in your career.

BOLLES: Are there a lot of such seminars?

GOLDBERG: Yes, there are. The basic theory is that underemployment is going to be a reality of the eighties and the nineties, so people should face the fact that they can only get fulfillment through hobbies and interests and think of their job as a way to make a living. What do you think of that?

BOLLES: It's difficult to criticize what they're saying because, like all ideas, there's some truth in it. During some of the recent decades, we've taught people that their work life was *the* thing that made them who they were and justified their existence. I don't think that's healthy, but the other side of it makes me a little uncomfortable too, because it tosses in the towel on the idea that you can get satisfaction in your work. That could turn out to be true, but I sure like to see everyone being adjured and exhorted to give it their best shot, to try to get work that is meaningful to them and is well suited to who they are.

GOLDBERG: I'm disappointed in your response. I thought you'd say, "Yes, you can get meaningful work," rather than, "You should give it a try, and then throw in the towel."

BOLLES: Only a magician would say everyone can find meaningful work. Suppose there were 104 million people who want work and 104 million jobs, and there were exactly the right number of jobs in each geographical area for the people who wanted them. I still could not sit here and try to claim that everyone would find just the job they want most, because when people go job hunting they bring a lot of other agendas with them.

GOLDBERG: Like what?

BOLLES: Suppose a woman's husband has seriously undermined her self-esteem. She's caught in a bind. She knows on one level that she's better than his concept of her, but on some other level, she wants his love and approval, and so she might feel that she has to live up to his low expectations. We'll frequently find that we can teach such people every single thing they need to know to conduct the job hunt successfully, yet they'll manage to botch it up.

GOLDBERG: The premise of this book is that a lot of energy is wasted by liberal arts graduates who believe that they have to get an advanced or technical degree. Isn't their time and energy better spent looking inside for what is meaningful to them and going after it?

BOLLES: Liberal arts graduates face a realization that goes something like this. They chose a certain kind of education because they wanted to find out what the world is like. It is likely that they have come to appreciate and be knowledgeable about a diversity of ideas and cultures and backgrounds—much more so than a person who had a more narrowly conceived college education. The price they pay for getting that kind of an education is that when it then comes time for them to look for a career, they will have to do some extra work right on the heels of their college education. That work is to struggle with this new decision, which their degree did not help them with, namely, "What is my greatest enthusiasm and where do I most want to work?" Technical students won't have to do that when they graduate, but they may well do it fifteen or twenty years later.

Since there are no real experts about where you should go with this degree and these skills, you've got to do some self-analysis and become your own expert. And nobody is better prepared for job hunting than the liberal arts graduate. The skills it takes to conduct a job hunt are the very skills the liberal arts graduate has been working on for four years in college.

GOLDBERG: What are the fatal mistakes of the people who fail at this process?

BOLLES: One fatal mistake is that they haven't done enough thinking about what it is they really want. They're going about looking for something that would please their mother, or their father, or the person they're in love with. They're still trying too hard to please other people instead of themselves.

Suppose you'd just graduated from college and I told you to go look for a job as a painter of swastikas on the sides of buildings. If you had any desire whatsoever to please me, you wouldn't dare tell me to go jump in the lake. You'd say, "All right, I'll go out and look for that job," but you'd figure out every way possible to botch up the search.

When you analyze why people don't get jobs, it turns out that lack of enthusiasm is the greatest factor. They may know how to job hunt, but if they're not looking for something they really want to find, it is in their psychological interest not to succeed.

GOLDBERG: Do you mean that if you *are* looking for a job you really want, you *can* find it?

BOLLES: That question brings us to the second mistake job hunters make, which is that they prematurely put a label on what it is they're seeking. They may say, "The only thing I'm interested in is being an interviewer for a major radio or television show." Well, there are a limited number of such jobs, and they may not get one. But suppose they asked themselves, "If I were an interviewer for a major radio or television show, what would give me my satisfactions about that job? How else could I get those same satisfactions? What else would let me use the same skills?"

GOLDBERG: Why don't people consider alternatives?

BOLLES: It's partly laziness, learned well during the liberal arts education. I've taught at a college, and I've ended up with a lot of people in my course because it was an easy five points. I didn't require much homework, I didn't grade that tough, and they were there not because the course fascinated them, but because they learned this was an easy way to get some more credits and get through the rest of college.

Once that habit is learned, it is transferable to the job hunt. The issue becomes, "How can I get through this as fast as possible, and with the least effort?" And one easy way to do that is to put an instant label on what they're looking for and say, "That's it. It has to be that. It can't be anything else."

GOLDBERG: Is the third mistake laziness?

BOLLES: No. The third mistake is that when they go to talk to people, they don't know what it is they're trying to find out.

I've had people come to see me and say, "So-and-so said if I was ever out this way, I should certainly look you up."

And I say, "Oh. Why?"

And they'll say, "He didn't exactly say why. He just said I should look you up."

And I say, "What is it you'd like me to be able to tell you or do for you?"

"Well, umm . . . I don't know, exactly, umm, do you know where there's a job?"

The whole idea of informational interviewing, as it's called, dissolves into what they think is a kind of routine method of magic. It's this belief in magic that does in so many job hunters. They think that if they go through a certain number of steps, described in *Parachute* or by a counselor or a best friend, they'll make it. Someone tells them, "You're suppose to go see a lot of people."

And they say, "Okay, I'll go see them."

If they do that just as an act of magic, they're not going to end up with a job unless they are miraculously lucky.

GOLDBERG: I wonder if you could add to this the concept of the moving sidewalk—that you get on a moving sidewalk in grammar school and stay on it through high school and through college, and then it takes you down the hall to the career counseling center and on to the General Motors interview, and so forth. And you just stand there.

BOLLES: The best thing liberal arts graduates should get out of their education is the realization that creativity is the most distinctive mark of anyone, regardless of I.Q. or any other considerations. When you job hunt, you're either going to go about it in a creative or an uncreative way, and to be creative in the job hunt means to think of every possible way of doing things. It means saying, "I'm going to go down this path, but if that doesn't work, I'm ready to try this other path."

When you talk to liberal arts graduates who are having trouble with their job hunt and you ask them what's wrong, they will often describe a course of action that would make the hair stand up on the back of your neck. For instance: "My uncle says that he heard that there's this place five miles down the road that he's just sure is going to have a vacancy next week. So, of course, I'm sitting at home reading Chaucer because I've got to wait until next week, and then I'm going down there and I'm going to get the job."

And you say, "What if your uncle is wrong and there is no vacancy, or what if somebody else gets it first?"

The answer: "Gee, I never thought of that."

If liberal arts graduates want to justify their degree they should justify it by being as creative as they can. And if you talk to people straight out of college, or twenty years later, who are doing the job hunt properly, you'll find they're actually having fun.

GOLDBERG: Why?

BOLLES: Because they're sharpening their teeth.

GOLDBERG: There's a mystery here. If you did well in college, enjoyed your liberal arts program, and have some idea about how to go about the job hunt, it would follow that you'd jump right into it and have a successful time of it. But we know that's often not the case. Why?

BOLLES: Part of the answer is that the world of work is not the same as the world of school; it's a whole new world.

GOLDBERG: Is it similar to what the returning homemaker faces?

BOLLES: Yes. The myth for years about the homemaker was that she or he, mostly she, had no "work" experience. That got dispelled by such organizations as Displaced Homemakers, Incorporated, and many women who had been homemakers have become aware of the fact that all the experience they'd had in the home over the years *was* work. There was a different kind of payment and a different series of rewards, but the work was just as real as if they'd been out in the marketplace all those years.

GOLDBERG: How about career switches? They should already be confident and comfortable in the work world and ready to go.

BOLLES: Oh, no, they're not! We're not talking about reality here, we're talking about their conception of reality. Let's take your occupation as a sterling example: we have a woman who has been a third-grade teacher, and she suddenly decides she wants to become an interviewer on a radio station. She may have been the most competent third-grade teacher in the western states, designated National Teacher of the Year. The fact that she's been at the top of her field will probably give her no confidence whatsoever when she goes into broadcasting. The old self-esteem simply deserts her and she feels like she's going into a new world. This is typical of career changers.

GOLDBERG: So then all three groups might be comforted to know that they share a lack of confidence as they get started.

BOLLES: When I was a child, we used to play a game called King of the Mountain. You'd be up on top of a hill about three feet above the sidewalk, and the goal was that everyone else would try to pull you down off that hill and get themselves up so that they would become King of the Mountain. That's what it's like in the world of work.

You're on top of the world in high school, and then you go to college and all of a sudden you're down at the bottom again. You get to the senior year in college, you're up at the top again, then you go into the work world and you're down at the bottom again. You rise in your career, and you're up at the top again, and then you change careers and suddenly you're at the bottom again. So there's an apprehension, which is what you're really asking about.

GOLDBERG: The technology of the eighties scares the heck out of a lot of liberal arts graduates. They say to themselves, "Oh my God, I'm about to go into the technological era and the job market that goes with it. I'm sunk!" Your response?

BOLLES: This is an era that is much worse for the blue-collar worker than ten or twenty years ago; it isn't the liberal arts graduate who is being phased out by the changes that are occurring in the labor market.

But besides the blue-collar worker, the position that will be most affected in times to come will be the manager, particularly the middle manager. If you look very carefully at that job, you'll see that the primary function is not to make decisions, but to be a center where information comes to rest and then is disbursed to people above and below. The age in which we live is going to eliminate the importance of this position, because information can flow directly from one person to another with a computer terminal. So I'd say if a liberal arts graduate is determined to become a manager, and a middle manager at that, then the age in which we live might pose a threat.

Apart from that, you hear the liberal arts graduate's future bandied about from decade to decade in terms of two labels: "generalist" and "specialist." People will say, "This is the time of the liberal arts graduate because what we want is generalists and that is what the liberal arts graduate is." And then you'll hear, "But this decade is not so hot for liberal arts graduates because what we need are specialists." Those generalizations are full of holes.

The real truth, of course, is that some places need generalists and the liberal arts graduate will be the ideal person for that role, and some places need certain kinds of specialists and the liberal arts graduate will be ideal for that kind of role. Other places need other kinds of specialists and the liberal arts graduate will *not* be ideal, so it varies greatly.

GOLDBERG: How would you compare opportunities for these two people? One says, "I'll take almost any job, just so long as it's not terrible, and at the same time I'll go out and look for a decent-paying professional job." The second is very fussy and waits for a job that's just right. Who's more likely to land the first great job?

BOLLES: The first person.

GOLDBERG: But I wouldn't want to hire someone who seems willing to take anything. I want someone who wants me.

BOLLES: You won't know that when you're hiring, if the applicant is good.

GOLDBERG: What about success? Can you pinpoint a common ingredient shared by successful job seekers?

BOLLES: The most common ingredient that we would find among successful job hunters is that they love what they're looking for. In other words, it's the enthusiasm. They have somehow gotten out of the victim mentality. They've gotten out of the idea that it doesn't matter what they want out of life and that they've got to settle for something so much less.

Successful job hunters have somehow, not in any formal pencil-and-paper sense, drawn up a new bill of rights for themselves. It says, "I have the right to work at something I care to do. I have the right to use the skills that I have spent some time mastering and perfecting, and the talents I was born with and which were gifts to me. I have the right to look at organizations and reject them if they aren't the sorts of places where I would like to be. I have the right to go after those organizations that *are* the kinds of places where I'd like to be."

In general, you could say that they've gone for an agricultural model of what a human being is rather than a technical engineering model. They do not see life as a series of mechanical steps, one gear turning another gear. Instead, they see themselves as a plant and they are really saying, "What's the environment where I would thrive the best, where I would grow the most?" They've essentially come up with that concept, though they might never articulate it that way.

GOLDBERG: Thank you for showing us a different dimension to the career search. You've shown us that there's no reason for liberal arts graduates to feel at a disadvantage. If anything, their training and their education give them a special advantage in a job search. Another point you've raised, an unexpected one, is the degree to which creativity is important in making this process not only successful, but more fun and more personally enriching.

CHAPTER 2

Look Inside Yourself

Initially, you have to believe that you have the right to, and deserve the right to, work at something that's going to make you happy. You're giving a lot of yourself to a job—physically, intellectually, emotionally. You're entitled to make an active choice. Therefore, the place you start is: "What would make me happy? Who am I?"

—*May Fraydas*

MAY FRAYDAS is the assistant director of Career Advising and Placement for liberal arts students at the University of Wisconsin in Madison. She and the other staff members at her office assist present and former students of the university through workshops, one-on-one counseling, information, and support. May herself is a veteran of a career switch, a "recycled school teacher," as she puts it. Six years ago, she faced up to some personal dissatisfactions with the teaching profession. For nine months, she taught a few nights a week to help make ends meet while she looked for a new position. She speaks with eloquence and conviction about the importance of personal satisfaction in a career.

GOLDBERG: Suppose you have a liberal arts degree, say a bachelor's in English. You went into college on the assumption that you were going to use that degree to teach English, to stay in academia, to stay in something directly related to that degree. Now either you can't find such a job, or you don't choose to have such a job. Can you find a career outside of academia?

FRAYDAS: Absolutely. However, one of the key issues for you is not to get hung up on your degree as a way of identifying who you are. One of the things that happens to people who have been in college a long or even a short time is that they put undue emphasis on the major. Employers are not nearly as interested in the major as they are in the person.

GOLDBERG: Then where does one begin? If you just got a degree, or you're about to get it, or even if you've had it for years and haven't used it, how do you begin to deal with the issue of jobs in the real world?

FRAYDAS: To be a fresh graduate with a liberal arts degree is a slightly different situation than to be a person who's had some life experience and a liberal arts degree. But generally speaking, you start by looking at what your skills are. Skills, plus what you want, what your values are, and what your goals are.

GOLDBERG: What I want to hear from you is: first, you do what you want to do. You just figure out what you'd like the most and that's the direction you take. I'm not hearing that.

FRAYDAS: I don't think that's totally untrue. In fact, one of the unfortunate aspects of a tight, competitive job market is that people don't even test what they want to do. They're so frightened they're not going to find a job that they try to please everyone. They try to become somebody else's ideal job candidate, instead of looking inside, instead of finding out who they are, what their strengths are, what they're good at, what turns them on, what stimulates them, and what they want to do. They don't even ask themselves these questions, and that's a big mistake.

GOLDBERG: I have a hunch that a lot of job hunters would just as soon have you tell them what to do. Instead, I hear you saying, "*They're* going to have to do some work."

FRAYDAS: It's a lot of work to find work. In fact, those people who do the search best often find more interesting jobs than people with the very best qualifications.

GOLDBERG: And they come out ahead of those who busted their chops throughout college?

FRAYDAS: In nontechnical fields that's true. In jobs that require an interdisciplinary approach to problem solving, communication, organization, and the ability to function as a generalist, they'll be ahead. And that's the kind of job most liberal arts people are going to be doing.

GOLDBERG: Getting back to "Go" in this career-hunting game, you're saying the first step is to take a look at yourself.

FRAYDAS: Yes. The process starts with the self. It moves to looking at the outside world in terms of career options, and then to finding a way to synthesize everything. "Who am I? What's out there? Where is there a fit?"

But first, I would examine my skills and my interests. One of the things that happens to us as adults is that we tend to be rewarded and reinforced for doing things that we're good at. And after a lot of years of that, we forget to ask ourselves if we like those things. You can be good at something, do it a lot and become experienced at it, but it may not be something that really fulfills you. One thing you can do is strip away those old self-concepts to the extent that you can and think about the things you've done in your life that you *really* liked and that *truly* absorbed you.

In this way, and as a place to start, you can use the past as a predictor of the future. Look at jobs, things you studied in school, things you did for fun, things you did in the community, with groups of people or alone. Then maybe you can come up with a few things and analyze them for what skills and what abilities and values were inherent in them.

GOLDBERG: It's not hard for people to think about things they've done in their lives that they chose to do rather than were made to do. Somebody might say, "Gee, I love racquetball," and he or she plays pretty well, but not at a pro level. Is that useful information?

FRAYDAS: Yes, I think so. Because aside from whatever athletic ability may be involved in the game, there are psychological reasons that we enjoy something like racquetball. Maybe we like competition. Maybe we like the setting and meeting of a goal. Maybe we like doing something under time constraints and are challenged by that. Maybe we have a high energy level. I really think that anything we've done can be looked at in terms of what it can tell us about ourselves.

GOLDBERG: I assume it's a little easier if you take things that are more obviously related to job skills. For example, if someone says, "You know, I always seem to be involved in political campaigns. I love to work for candidates," it tells you something much more specific.

FRAYDAS: I think the key word in that statement is *always*.

Everything we've ever liked may not be significant; what becomes significant are the patterns that emerge.

GOLDBERG: Suppose I had come to see you when I was twenty-five and had been out of college for a couple of years. At that point I had no media background. Do you think I might have discovered that I longed to be an interviewer?

FRAYDAS: That may have come through in our conversation on some intuitive level. But what's more likely to have come through is a general sense of what parts of yourself you wanted to use. Let me give you an example. Very often, when you ask people to talk about the kind of fantasy job they imagine themselves having and some of their distinctive qualities that might relate to that, one of the things they'll say is, "I love people." But that means nothing, because we all, if we live on planet Earth, interact with people in one way or another no matter what job we have.

What becomes important is to define the ways in which you like to work with people. Perhaps you like to teach people, or supervise them, or motivate them, or sell things to them, or train them. Maybe you like to evoke responses from them, counsel them, give them advice, take out their appendix. General statements are okay to start with, but then you really need to refine them. It's not always easy to do this alone, but people can get help with this kind of self-research in most communities.

GOLDBERG: Through what kinds of sources?

FRAYDAS: Typically, if there's a university anywhere around, there will be a career-advising office, and certainly that office can be helpful in many ways. There are also some very useful tests. The Strong-Campbell Interest Inventory, for example, looks at your interests and correlates them with those of people already in certain professions. There are probably community groups in most areas that can help with this process; the chamber of commerce might well know about career-related workshops in the community.

An individual who feels comfortable sharing that kind of information with other people, and having a facilitator, can look for some of these more structured options. People who hate groups can get a book like *What Color Is Your Parachute?* or have a conversation with a good friend or a partner and just talk about some of this stuff. But you do need to do some of it on paper and you do need to do some of it in a formal way or at least start to approach it that way.

GOLDBERG: But it's really hard to look inside yourself and say, "What do I really like? What am I really good at?"

FRAYDAS: It's extremely hard. That's why I think people should do it with the help of somebody else. We live in a society that doesn't encourage us to articulate our own strengths very directly. Other people are more likely to give us credit for our skills.

GOLDBERG: Can you think of someone you counseled and describe what that person learned about him or herself and what kind of career he or she wound up in? I'd like to get a feel for how this process works.

FRAYDAS: I can invent a person for you. Let's talk about a college senior who has a major in English and has been doing a lot of research papers and creative writing for school. Let's say he works for a fast-food chain to make money on a part-time basis and has appeared in a couple of plays.

GOLDBERG: How can he translate those experiences and interests into skill categories?

FRAYDAS: Let's look at the academic aspect first: the research, the papers, the reading. What does it mean to know how to write a paper, for example? It means that you know how to conceptualize an idea, that you know how to collect and analyze data and how to articulate your findings in some written form. You probably also know how to draw some conclusions based on those findings. That's an example of identifying skills in a more general way, even from something as specific as writing an academic paper.

GOLDBERG: And, of course, the person you're talking with is feeling very good about all the skills and strengths he's discovered he has.

FRAYDAS: Right! And he's amazed!

GOLDBERG: But he's also thinking, "So what? I can write and assemble information. That's wonderful, but *I need a job*."

FRAYDAS: Of course, there has to be a bridge built between that first step and a job. But first, it's no small thing to convince a college graduate that he or she really does have marketable skills. Once you've got someone thinking that way, it becomes a lot easier to talk about how to express those skills in a form that an employer will recognize: a resumé, an interview. Furthermore, talking about those skills can lead you to identify career areas. For example, if you're terrific at writing and theater, and you're a terrific communicator, you probably ought to work in some form of communications.

GOLDBERG: Like what?

FRAYDAS: Maybe publishing, or journalism, or a media job, or sales. Sales is definitely a career that requires all sorts of communications skills.

GOLDBERG: Let's say you're talking to someone who has a degree in engineering, but doesn't want to be an engineer at all. And she says, "I've got a degree in engineering and I'm good at it, but I don't like it. What I really want to do is write." Could she go into publishing?

FRAYDAS: Sure, although my first impulse would be to try to find a compromise between the training and the love. Technical writing for an engineer would be a good example of that, a way to marry those two extremely different areas.

People think they have to either limit themselves to their training or totally throw it away. But we're all multidimensional, and we can probably find ways to combine our educational focus with our other interests. I think we create false distinctions when we educate people. It's really for the convenience of the bureaucracies of the world that we need these labels.

GOLDBERG: Are you saying that people have more career options than they generally believe?

FRAYDAS: People who are bright, who learn quickly, who are enthusiastic and energetic, who are able to solve problems and organize the world they live in, who give of themselves, who have a sense of fun and excitement, and who are willing to create situations—these people can do anything they want to do!

Of course, this is easier if you're unemcumbered by other people who are relying on you for income and that sort of thing. I'm presenting a scenario for a person who need care only about him or herself in the process.

GOLDBERG: You've seen thousands of people with bachelor's degrees, some just graduating, others who've been out there a while. What kind of jobs do people with, for example, a bachelor's degree in English wind up with?

FRAYDAS: I know a young woman with a degree in English whose husband was going to law school in New York City. She was from a very small town, had never left Wisconsin, and she was terrified. But within three weeks, I got a note from her. She was working in the research department of an advertising agency and they were going to be promoting her to a more interesting position. She had started out with perseverance and some communication skills. She had pounded the sidewalk, knocked on people's doors, talked to them face-to-face. She had been willing to start out in a less-than-glamorous position, and she had learned well.

GOLDBERG: Was it her persistence that pulled her through?

FRAYDAS: That was part of it. But also, she was willing to take risks and be flexible. People who think that today is forever, that the first job has to be Prince Charming and whisk them off to total happiness forever are the ones who often have the hardest time finding an interesting job.

GOLDBERG: At five years old, you enter the school system. And if you're graduating with your bachelor's degree, you've been told what to do for almost your entire life or you've been given clear choices: do you want A, B, or C? And now, suddenly, you have to examine things yourself and make your own decisions. There's no multiple choice in the real world, and I think that can be a hard adjustment for students to make.

FRAYDAS: You've really hit on something significant. Most of the students I see fit a certain stereotype: if they could go down next fall and register for a happy life, they would do it. They'd just say, "Where do I sign?"

People in our society are not trained to become individuals or to test who they are, except in the terms that are already laid out. Very often they only do it in times of crisis, when they have to; but once they learn how, they can't turn back. Once you've had a taste of that kind of freedom, even though it may be painful and scary, you will always want to be responsible for your own life.

GOLDBERG: Taking charge and knowing yourself.

FRAYDAS: Being willing *not* to do wonderfully, to fail, to make some mistakes, to be a jerk.

GOLDBERG: How does that help?

FRAYDAS: Sometimes the people who have the most difficulty with a problem are the people who have always done things well: the very competent, bright people who always got A's in school, who were always elected president of every organization and never had a broken love affair. Those are the people who can really get thrown by a difficult situation. The rest of the world—most of us—have learned from a very early age that you have to reshift things and adapt and give some things up and try for new things.

GOLDBERG: Let's talk about personalities. How important is it for the job hunter to think about his or her personality?

FRAYDAS: Very important. I would like to use the word *values*, though, rather than *personality*.

You have to pay attention to how you really feel and how you respond to all the things that are involved in your environment at any given time. For instance, how does it feel to have someone tell you what to do?

I have a friend who, no matter what job he's had or who his supervisor has been, has always hated his supervisor. He hates that relationship; he doesn't like to be told what to do. That's someone who shouldn't be working for someone else. That person should be working for himself.

Other people like to have someone come along and say, "Gee, what you just did is terrific," or, "How about doing it this way?" They need that reinforcement.

These are aspects of work situations that have to do with our personalities, and they are seldom articulated until we're on the job. By then it's often too late to have control over them.

GOLDBERG: How do we look at our personality? Other than looking at our skills and abilities, how do we assess our being, our values, our essence?

FRAYDAS: First, it's important to look at who we are in our personal lives and not make an arbitrary distinction between who we are and what we want there, and who we are and what we want from our working relationships.

If we need and like a lot of intimacy in our personal relationships, we would probably be comfortable working with other people and having them react to our work. Maybe we want to be doing work that by definition is *about* people reacting to our work, for example counseling or interviewing.

Or we might be people who are most comfortable with privacy and solitude, in which case our work situation should reflect that. If we don't like messy things that involve interpretation, but prefer things to either be true or false, maybe we should be working with statistics, data, or science; maybe we should be working in a lab or with a computer. That's the kind of world we find reassuring or interesting.

GOLDBERG: You also deal with people who may be a little negative about the business world, but who are going through a transformation, either as they graduate or later in life. Any words of wisdom for these people about dealing with what may feel to them like selling out?

FRAYDAS: There's a phenomenon these days of the person who not only has a bachelor's degree in liberal arts, but also a graduate degree in a specialized field, and who cannot find a job. An example would be a person who has a Ph.D. in Italian renaissance literature who can't or doesn't want to find a job in academia, is thirty years old, has children and debts. That person may be bitter, resentful, perhaps frightened, and may not see the business world as reflecting his or her values.

A lot of these people are doing one of two things: either going into retraining programs for Ph.D's, which are very popular, short programs with maybe a couple of business courses and some related things, or they're being trained by industry. They're coming back and saying, "I've never been happier." It's amazing.

GOLDBERG: I would have guessed that they might feel disappointed that they're not using their specialized training.

FRAYDAS: First, they're getting a good salary. That sounds crass, but for someone who has never really been concretely rewarded and who has a lot of debts, which is true for most graduate students, it makes a tremendous difference. It gives these people adulthood and control over their lives on a level that they've never had before.

Also, they're feeling stimulated, they're surprised by how many bright people are out there, and by how, in fact, they need to be on their toes and producing their best work. And finally, they're not in a vacuum, but in the real world.

GOLDBERG: If you have a college degree, at whatever level, and you want to find a first job or switch careers or return to the work force after years of being a homemaker, can you find a satisfying career without being retooled by returning to school?

FRAYDAS: Absolutely. In fact, as long as people don't depend exclusively on their academic major to define who they are, they have a world of opportunities. They only have to get to *who they are* in terms of their skills, their experience, their abilities, and their values. Those things are much more significant to an employer than an academic degree.

GOLDBERG: Can you give us an overview? Where does one begin in this self-assessment process and how does one follow through?

FRAYDAS: Initially, you have to believe that you have the right to work at something that's going to make you happy. You're giving a lot of yourself to a job—physically, intellectually, emotionally. You're entitled to make an active choice. Therefore, the place you start is: "What would make me happy? Who am I?"

And then, of course, there has to be some aspect of reality. It's not just, "What's going to make me happy?" but, "What do I realistically have the skills, experience, history, abilities, and training to do?"

GOLDBERG: And you see getting assistance with this as critical?

FRAYDAS: It's very difficult to do it in a vacuum. You feel isolated, you may not be very accurate, and you may not be perceiving yourself very well. It's lonely. It's depressing.

There's a lot of support available both from people who are going through the same process and from so-called experts.

GOLDBERG: And I assume that going through this process not only helps your career development, but also helps you know yourself more fully and feel better about yourself.

FRAYDAS: Absolutely.

GOLDBERG: A final summary: the first step in a hunt for a job that will be truly satisfying is a long and honest look at who you are, through an examination of your experiences, your interests, and your skills. Schoolwork and past employment are important to assess, but don't overlook other areas: hobbies, community activities, sports, your interpersonal style. This kind of thorough examination will give you a good indication not only of the kind of jobs you'd succeed with, but also the kind of jobs you'd enjoy.

CHAPTER 3

Make Your Resumé
Work for You

Typically, a resumé will get less than ten seconds of the recruiter's time. Something in it has to reach out, grab him by
the throat, and convince him to go back to it and carefully
go over the whole thing.

—*Kirby Stanat*

KIRBY STANAT, through a remarkable variety of mediums, has
aided and influenced thousands of job hunters. He has re-
cruited for major industry, written a widely syndicated column
called "Chasing a Career," and directed both the Placement
Office and the Associated Union Services at the University of
Wisconsin at Milwaukee. Mr. Stanat is also the author of *Job
Hunting Secrets and Tactics*, a book now in its third printing,
with over 65,000 copies sold. He is president of his own executive search firm, and his television series, "Stanat on Jobs," has
been seen on forty-four stations around the country.

GOLDBERG: May Fraydas has given us some ideas about how to look
inside ourselves and reorient our thinking toward a new career.
Among other things, she stressed the importance of assessing our
abilities, our life patterns, our experience, and our values. The next
step is to put all that down in writing: to write a resumé.

Why are we even talking about resumés? Do they really matter?

STANAT: A resumé is one of the most important documents any
individual will ever produce. When I interview candidates for a

29

job, they are asking me to buy them. And if the job pays $15,000 a year with 20 percent fringe benefits tacked on top, we're looking at an $18,000 yearly investment. You don't sell an $18,000 product with a ten-cent vehicle. So, the resumé is extraordinarily important.

GOLDBERG: How is it used by the employer?

STANAT: It arrives in a stack. When I was with Litton Industries, for instance, I would get stacks that would equal maybe four Sears catalogs every week. Your resumé is in the middle of a stack like that, and it's important for you to know that typically a resumé will get less than ten seconds of a recruiter's time. The resumé that is poorly constructed or poorly printed, that doesn't feel good or look good, is abandoned even more quickly than that.

Ordinarily, the resumé is the first thing that the recruiter sees of you, and something in it has to reach out and grab him by the throat and convince him to go back to it and carefully go over the whole thing.

GOLDBERG: Let's talk about the nitty-gritty of writing this resumé. First, what should it look like physically? The color of the paper, size, number of pages . . .

STANAT: No one deserves a resumé that's any longer than two pages. That's it.

GOLDBERG: Why?

STANAT: I won't read it. I have too many to go through. You can bring supporting information along to an interview.

GOLDBERG: What is your response to the person who says, "But my life is more important than two pages."

STANAT: "I don't care. Next?" That's pretty much what happens with a resumé. I have received resumé documents that should have been delivered by UPS, and I just don't have time for that. As a matter of fact, everything you want me to know about you should be on the first page.

GOLDBERG: Why?

STANAT: Because if I find nothing of interest on the first page, I will certainly find nothing of interest on the second page, and it will be discarded.

The first page should contain your personal information and it should go beyond what is truly legal for an employer to ask. On my resumé, I put down height, weight, age, marital status, home telephone, business telephone, address, and a statement about health. That's the personal data.

GOLDBERG: Can an employer ask about health?

STANAT: Yes, but it's a very awkward question. "Do you have any health conditions that might affect a job assignment?" Something like that. So I'm going to volunteer it. And if I were thirty years younger I would put down something about my military status.

GOLDBERG: Why?

STANAT: Because some people have a reserve commitment. If there's a military obligation or a military obligation has been completed, the employer should know.

GOLDBERG: What do employers think when they see that you've listed all this personal information that most other people don't list?

STANAT: The employer thinks, "This individual is open and forthright and has nothing to hide."

GOLDBERG: What's next?

STANAT: A statement about my education, with the most important educational credentials heading that up. If I'm a graduate of the University of Wisconsin, that's going to be the first listing. If I have a master's degree, that will be the first listing, with my undergraduate degree coming after that. If my most important education has been high school, that's what I would list. If you have college, you needn't list high school.

GOLDBERG: What about people who have been to five different colleges. Should they list them all and the credits they took?

STANAT: What I'm after is where the degree was granted, so they should construct a sentence that says that they attended these other colleges before graduating from the University of Wisconsin, or wherever. And the credits are not necessary.

GOLDBERG: So don't make the employer work hard; make it easy to get the basics.

STANAT: Yes. Remember that you have just ten seconds of my time.

GOLDBERG: Okay. After personal data and education?

STANAT: There are probably about six inches of page one left to work with, and this space should be devoted to most recent work experience. I'm a recruiter, and if I want to continue being a recruiter, I will use a great many details and numbers to describe my recruiting experience: "I hired X number of people in these salary ranges over this period of years." Numbers are neat and we respond well to them.

That's page one. The second page is the rest of my life. All other jobs go here. If I have been promoted from one position in a company to my present position, even that past job with the same employer goes on the second page. I list it as a separate job, with the company stuck out there in the left-hand margin just as you always do. As you read, you'll see my present employer's name appears twice, with the statement "Reason for leaving: promoted to the above position."

GOLDBERG: If you've had five jobs, should you state a reason for leaving each one?

STANAT: Yes.

GOLDBERG: And that's a column you have running down?

STANAT: Yes.

GOLDBERG: And the left-hand column is the name of the firm or agency you work for?

STANAT: Let's follow it across. At the top of my work experience I'm going to put "Litton Industries," with the address immediately underneath. Next to "Litton Industries" will be columns for POSITION ("Personnel Manager"), and DATES OF EMPLOYMENT ("1982 to present"). Underneath my position is the name of my supervisor and his or her phone number.

Now I skip a line and write a job description. It's comfortable for me to write in the third person, so my job description will say, "Mr. Stanat did this" or "Mr. Stanat did that."

GOLDBERG: Why the third person?

STANAT: That's my style. Other people may be more comfortable with "I."

GOLDBERG: Should you use whichever you're most comfortable with?

STANAT: Yes. And the sentences needn't be complete.

GOLDBERG: What if the job description is a complicated one? Is it okay to take three of four lines to describe your job?

STANAT: It should take far more than that.

GOLDBERG: I don't understand. You've said that the employer doesn't have time to read anything at length, yet you're suggesting a long job description.

STANAT: Of the present duties only.

GOLDBERG: And on page two, how much detail should you provide about previous jobs?

STANAT: The next most recent job gets half the space of the first one, and the next one gets half again, and so forth. When I talk about a job that I had fifteen years ago, that's one sentence. Fifteen years ago is ancient history. Who cares?

GOLDBERG: What comes next on page two?

STANAT: Probably not very much, unless you think it's important. I don't really care what your hobbies are, although a lot of people list them, and they may have interest to some. You may tell me that you're willing to relocate.

GOLDBERG: How about awards?

STANAT: If you've done something outside of your employment that relates to how you might fit into the community as well as the workplace, you might tell me about it. You could tell me that you're active in your church or in scouting—things like that.

GOLDBERG: What about references?

STANAT: Your present supervisor or immediate past supervisor is the most important reference. Beyond that, references ordinarily have little value.

GOLDBERG: But what about people who don't want their boss to know they're searching?

STANAT: If you do not want to have your present employer contacted, simply say, "Please do not contact the present employer without my permission." I have never known that to be violated.

GOLDBERG: Is the recruiter suspicious if there's no one to call for a reference?

STANAT: No, not really. The modern way to do it is to use as a final sentence "References available upon request."

GOLDBERG: Is it helpful to list personal references or references who might be relevant to a particular employer?

STANAT: If it's very early in your career and you don't have much more to present, that can be helpful. But ordinarily, if you've been around for a while, those aren't very important.

GOLDBERG: You haven't included career objectives anywhere in this resumé. Why?

STANAT: I think a statement about career objectives should be in a cover letter. That way, you can target the career objective to the particular job opening. If you put it on the resumé, it has to be a very general statement, and it loses its impact.

GOLDBERG: What else goes in the cover letter?

STANAT: The title of the job for which you're applying and your salary level. You could say, "My current salary is $18,000," or "I am seeking a position at a salary level of——." In either case, the employer knows that he or she will have to at least match your present salary or be in the ball park of your desired salary to be attractive.

GOLDBERG: Anything else?

STANAT: A statement of availability. For example, "I can be available two weeks following the negotiations." That's about it.

GOLDBERG: Any tips on the physical form the cover letter should take?

STANAT: It should be very brief. It *must* be an original. I get cover letters all the time that have been mass-produced with things filled in, and they are atrocious. These people aren't making much of an effort.

GOLDBERG: Let's say you read an ad in the paper for a marketing position at Kohler Plumbing. You decide to get the attention of the head of personnel, so your first paragraph says, "I've always admired your company, and I like your community, etc." Paragraph two says, "I am available as such and such a date, at such and such a salary, and I am looking for a position exactly as described."

Wouldn't it ingratiate you more with the employer to add that personal touch?

STANAT: Perhaps, but I think that most recruiters are cynical people. It's hard to stroke us in a resumé or a cover letter.

GOLDBERG: You've said that a recruiter will only spend about ten seconds on a resumé. What kind of attention will a cover letter be given?

STANAT: I scan them. And they are important. If you grab me with the cover letter, you'll force me to spend some time with the resumé. Then, if the resumé interests me, the cover letter becomes an integral part of the whole package.

GOLDBERG: As you scan the cover letter, what do you look for?

STANAT: I look for buzz words—a job title or a salary figure—or I look for a kill factor. If I don't have any $40,000 jobs, there's no need to pursue that application. It's simply out.

You might also grab me in other ways. I suggest to people that they use an extremely high-quality paper, paper that a printer says has a good "hand" to it. The paper should be off-white or white, no garish colors.

GOLDBERG: Why not gray or soft yellow or something like that?

STANAT: That would be fine, but magenta is not going to do the job for me. And a cover letter *must* be neatly typed.

GOLDBERG: Can you do it on any typewriter, or should you use a high-class office typewriter.

STANAT: You're better off using a high-quality office typewriter. And the type that comes out as script is often counterproductive.

GOLDBERG: Do you suggest typesetting the resumé?

STANAT: You can copy it if the copy process produces a clean, black, good-looking document. And have somebody proofread it for you. I recently placed a vice-president of engineering in a firm in Milwaukee; this man had sent me a resumé with an incorrect phone number. Because of his credentials, and because of the position I was trying to fill, I took the time and the effort to track him down. But if I'm looking at a more junior position and I get a wrong phone number, it's all over.

If you have moved, redo the resumé. The ones that are edited by hand are unacceptable. And spelling must be correct. I get tired of talking to people who want to work in "personal." It's very good strategy to ask a friend to read your resumé for completeness and accuracy, and then ask, "Do you understand what I said in my resumé?"

GOLDBERG: Would you discuss the "functional" versus the "chronological" resumé? In what situations would you use one rather than the other?

STANAT: When you want to continue in your current course, the chronological resumé permits you to put the most pertinent information on the front page. You go to the functional resumé when you are changing careers. Again, the goal is to get everything you want the recruiter to know about you on the front page. Since a chronological resumé won't work in this case, you bring the pertinent, functional information up front and say, "This is what I have done or what I want to do that relates to my new, chosen career."

Everything is the same on these two types of resumés down through education. But in the last third of the page, you describe interests, skills, direction, and ambitions. And it probably works best as a paragraph of prose.

Functional resumés are difficult to create, and in my opinion they are seldom very effective. Functional resumés and career changes are not traditional, and we all know what happens with untraditional things: people are afraid of them. That includes recruiters.

GOLDBERG: Let me give you a hypothetical situation and ask you to design a resumé. Our example is a woman who's been teaching seventh grade, but who's always been interested in commodities trading. She's been successful in trading commodities herself and now wants a job with a firm that's in the commodities business. What does she put on the bottom third of her first page?

STANAT: In a functional resumé, she'll put down those things that apply directly to the position she's applying for. Perhaps she's played the commodities market herself. Perhaps she's been trained, so that she can be licensed quickly. Perhaps she has an interest in a particular area of commodities. She can point these things out as functions that she has performed or has been trained to perform that will directly relate to a career in commodities.

GOLDBERG: The employer is going to look at all this personal information and think, "My gosh, this person is thirty-nine years old, and I don't see a job here. I see a bunch of things that she's interested in and some things she's done, but I don't see a career." Isn't that going to be disturbing to the employer?

STANAT: A career is going to show up on the second page, because somewhere down the line she's going to have to state that she's been a teacher. So the employer suddenly discovers that this is a teacher who's seeking a career change, and it's awkward. There's no question that career changes are tough, and they require a lot of selling by the candidate.

GOLDBERG: You mentioned that you should not write a resumé on paper that's a little wild in color or form. How then do you get your resumé noticed if it's part of a stack of two hundred?

STANAT: It doesn't take much for that resumé to jump out of the stack. High-quality paper will give the message that this individual has taken some time, has spent some money, is presenting him or herself in a very professional fashion. A resumé that's constructed well, is accurate, and appears on high-quality paper is in itself unusual.

GOLDBERG: Let me summarize the points we've discussed: use the chronological resumé form if possible. Functional resumés are appropriate when switching careers, but they are hard to construct effectively. The cover letter is important and should include the title of the job being applied for and salary expectations. The resumé should be no longer than two pages and most of the information important to the employer should be right on page one. The more you tell the employer about yourself in that resumé, the more comfortable the employer will be in working with you.

CHAPTER 4

The Hidden Job Market

About 80 percent of the job market is *not* accounted for by the best-known sources: want ads and employment agencies. Then how *do* you find out about these jobs?
—*Dick Goldberg*

MARY KAUPFER and TOM JOHNSON approach the subject of job hunting from the very realistic perspective afforded by decades of experience in career guidance and placement. Mary Kaupfer has owned an employment agency for more than twenty years. During that time, she has placed thousands of clients in corporate, administrative, and clerical positions. Tom Johnson is the director of the Career Guidance and Placement Office at the University of Wisconsin at Madison, a service that advises students in the university's liberal arts programs. Before that he was a recruiter for both a major advertising company and a Fortune 500 company.

GOLDBERG: When most people begin looking for a job, the first thing that comes to mind is opening a newspaper and looking in the want ads. Is that a good place for the liberal arts graduate to begin looking for a career?

JOHNSON: It's *a* place to begin looking. I don't think it's the most effective place. Many of the companies and organizations that advertise for people via want ads are really looking for experienced people, and most recent college graduates come to the work force without relevant work experience.

KAUPFER: Also, want ads really only list about 8 percent of all the

37

available positions. And according to the statistics, employment agencies in the United States fill only about 5 percent. Another 5 percent are placed by job services. So that leaves a great many people looking for and getting jobs through friends of friends and contacts.

GOLDBERG: Then about 80 percent of the job market is *not* accounted for by the best-known sources: want ads and employment agencies. Just how *do* you find out about these jobs? Specifically, how can the liberal arts graduate find these jobs?

JOHNSON: The most effective way is by using a network of personal contacts. It takes a bit of work, but a student or graduate can develop these contacts, and they can be extremely important.

Also, I would like to state unequivocally that having a degree in the humanities is not a liability. It's my impression that employers in nontechnical fields are looking for people with the skills that are, if not peculiar to the humanities graduate, certainly found in the humanities graduate. Specifically, these are people who have a good sense of direction, extremely well-developed communication skills, and the ability to organize, to plan, to analyze, to do research, and to discover new ways of looking at old problems.

The biggest problem for humanities graduates is not the employer, but themselves. They have to learn to be confident about what they know and what they can do, and they have to spend some time researching opportunities and identifying their skills. Then they must be able to articulate the relevancy of those skills to a particular job. If they can do that, they'll be in good shape.

KAUPFER: I agree with everything Tom said. It's a question of really seeking and finding those openings, and liberal arts graduates have every bit as much of an opportunity to do that as anyone else, provided they *want* to do it.

I do quite a bit of counseling with people who are just beginning to look for a career, and I find that they're in something of a "comfort zone." They've been going to school, and for the most part, it's a very pleasant environment, and they've gotten kind of used to it. Suddenly they're thrown out into the work force. They're not in that comfort zone anymore, and panic sets in.

I also find that people tend to be a little lazy. They don't go far enough in finding out what they're really like or what types of jobs are available for them.

GOLDBERG: So we get back to the importance of self-assessment. People don't seem to want to do that work. Why?

KAUPFER: I'm not sure that they really understand what it's going to take to make a thorough self-assessment. Even if they do, they just may not want to take the time.

It's very simple for a young man or woman to complete a course in computer science and go into programing and systems work, or for a marketing major to move into a product-development career. But a liberal arts graduate wonders, "Now, what's available for me?" And the answer, of course, is determined to a great extent by the amount of energy he or she puts into the career search.

JOHNSON: That's a key point. However, I would prefer to describe that behavior as "passive" instead of "lazy." I have clients who come into my office and say, "I am graduating with a major in such and such. What kind of jobs are available for me?" I think they're really going about the process backward. The question should be, "I have these kind of skills, these kind of values, these kinds of interests. Where can I put them to work?"

GOLDBERG: These seem to be recurring themes: don't be passive; look into yourself; look into the world.

JOHNSON: That's right. Those are keys. And I think the best approach, and in the long run the most effective approach, is what's referred to as "informational interviewing."

There are two types of interviewing connected with the job search: that which you do for information about different careers and companies, and that which you do with an employer to get a job. Informational interviewing is the first.

If I were interested in advertising, for instance, I would try to identify people who were in the advertising field. I would give them a call and say, "Hey, I'm not looking for a job—I want you to understand that right away—but I am thinking about entering your profession. I would very much like to meet with you and talk about what you do, how you do it, the kinds of people you look for in your company, and generally what your job is all about."

When we do this, we make a contact. Shortly afterward, a thank-you note should be sent and a resumé can be enclosed. The note can include a statement along the general line of: "As a result of our conversation, I've decided that advertising is what I want to do. Your thoughts helped reinforce this decision, and I would like to chat with you now about a job. I'm enclosing a copy of my resumé. Can you suggest how I might best . . ."

GOLDBERG: Isn't this person going to think that you're a creep because you promised when you called that you just wanted information and weren't looking for a job?

KAUPFER: Not at all.

JOHNSON: No. I'm suggesting that this takes place after the informational interview.

GOLDBERG: But your contact will think you were devious, that you really knew all along that you were going to ask for a job.

JOHNSON: I don't think so. If I received a letter like the one I described, I would be flattered and pleased that I had some influence upon this person's decision. No, I don't think the person would be turned off.

I would issue this caveat, however: one thing that you should never take to the informational interview is a copy of your resumé. Halfway through the interview, you might be inclined to whip it out. Then the person *will* feel suckered.

GOLDBERG: What about the person who thinks, "I can't do that. I don't have the nerve to pick up the phone and make that kind of call." Even with the reassurance you've offered, they're still worried that they'll hear, "What do you want? Don't you know I'm busy?"

JOHNSON: All of us like to talk about what we do. I probably receive four or five requests a semester from people who are considering career placement as a profession, or who are interested in advertising and ask me to talk with them about my days at the agency. I love to do that.

If I'm enjoying myself, I'm likely to like you. I had a recruiter tell me once that people simply hire people they like. If you have fifty applicants for a job, you never end up with forty-nine who obviously do not fit and one magical person who does. You end up with perhaps four or five who fit, and the person who is eventually hired will be the one the employer feels will best fit the image of the organization and the department and the one with whom he or she feels most compatible. That's why I think dress and mannerisms in the interview are incredibly important.

GOLDBERG: So you're saying not to go to the informational interview just to get information; but to be someone you're proud to be.

JOHNSON: Certainly one of the objectives in the informational interview is to get information, but the hidden agenda item should be to try to create a favorable impression.

GOLDBERG: Besides the chance that this person can find you a job when you send a resumé a couple of weeks later, how else can he or she help you?

JOHNSON: That first contact is probably not involved in the job-selection process. The most he or she can do is put you in touch with the person who's going to be making the hiring decision.

KAUPFER: Consider that first contact a resource.

JOHNSON: For example, the agency that I was with many years ago got a vast amount of mail every day. I would go through that pile, and periodically there would be a resumé that came from someone down in Traffic or Copy. There would be a little note attached: "Tom, I received this resumé from an alumnus at my school. I had coffee with him last week. Would you please give this resumé a little attention?" You can be sure I read that resumé a lot more closely because it came from someone within the organization.

The last questions that I would have for my informational contact would be: "Do you know other people in the business that I can talk to? If so, may I use your name as an introduction?"

GOLDBERG: Do you suggest using telephone informational interviews?

JOHNSON: I much prefer the face-to-face interview. Once again, one of the things you want to accomplish is to let the person know that you dress well and carry yourself well. That's hard to do over the phone.

GOLDBERG: Let's say we've done eight informational interviews. They've gone well, we've gotten lots of information, we've sent resumés later and hoped that they would be directed to someone involved in the hiring process. We've done everything right and . . . nothing happens. What other avenues can we pursue?

KAUPFER: First, I wouldn't let it stop there. I probably would get back to those individuals at some point. You need to remind your resource people that you're out there, because after all, they are busy. They might have said, "Sure, I'd be glad to help you. No problem at all." And then suddenly a big project came up and even if they really did know about a job, they just didn't have time to get back to you.

You can call and say, "I really appreciated the help. Is there anything that you may have heard of by this time?" You don't want to be a pest, so make it short. But I do think you should follow up these contacts.

JOHNSON: The trick is to be active, not passive, in the job search.

KAUPFER: Also, you're assuming eight interviews are enough. I don't think you can stop there. Look at the interviews not only as informational, but as a way to develop the contacts you're going to need.

JOHNSON: The informational interview is a primary way to do this, but there are others. Alumni contacts can be very important. If I had graduated recently and were looking for a job, I would find the alumni club in my area, contact its president, and say, "I'm a graduate from the University of Wisconsin. I'm not calling to ask you for a job, but I hope you can tell me if there's anyone in the club who's in the advertising business and who I might contact." That's a little easier than just calling someone on the phone and asking cold.

I would also consider contacting a placement office like ours at UW. We have any number of contacts, including firms that recruit from us, and often we can identify recent alumni in your geographical area or in the career field you're interested in.

If there are faculty members with whom you were relatively close, another tactic might be to ask if they know of people you can contact, and whether you might use their names as a way of introduction. Many faculty members do consulting and have contacts in industry.

Consider contacts within your religious organization, if you belong to one. A congregation is one of the most eclectic groups of people imaginable, with doctors and plumbers and carpenters and bank presidents. Fraternities, sororities, and activity clubs can help you identify contacts, and so can undergraduate advisers. Certain professions have national and regional associations connected with them, for example the American Personnel Association and the American Association of Advertising Agencies.

KAUPFER: Parents of friends can be extremely important.

JOHNSON: Yes. And so can friends of parents. Also there are job clubs throughout the country, and they can be really wonderful.

GOLDBERG: How do you find them?

JOHNSON: There are several ways. You can check with the placement office of a college or with a religious or social service organization. A state unemployment service can provide you with a list.

But do try to have names and contacts. If you just pull out the phone book and call ten advertising agencies or ten anything, you should expect a fair amount of rejection.

GOLDBERG: I would assume big cities are a lot easier to network in than smaller communities.

JOHNSON: Generally speaking, that's true.

KAUPFER: The disadvantage of a smaller city is that you might stay with a position for two years and find that the company just has not given you the opportunity to advance that you need. Then it requires relocation to get another job in the same profession. Larger cities generally do have more opportunities, though you really have to look at the statistics on unemployment to determine which cities are viable for you.

GOLDBERG: How can you explore San Diego's job opportunities in your field without moving there?

JOHNSON: Except for the person with a high-tech major, it's much easier to find a job if you're on-site. Suppose you're in Nebraska and an employer in San Diego has an opening in your chosen field. Suppose, also, that there are fifteen local candidates for the position. Is the employer going to spend the money to fly you in for an interview on the chance that you're better than the local candidates? Do *you* want to spend the money to fly out without knowing what your chances are?

KAUPFER: You really have to be very careful before you pick up and move. However, if you are relocating, there are some things that can be done ahead of time that will help in a job search.

Libraries almost always have telephone directories and Yellow Pages of larger cities. Often they also have the Sunday edition of major city newspapers, and even though the classifieds only list about 8 percent of available jobs, they do give you a feel for the area. Many libraries also have an industrial directory, which will give you an idea of the types of industries in different areas. And if you're going into advertising, for example, you could pretty well determine what type of advertising might be in a given area just from the types of industry that exist there.

JOHNSON: When people move to a new area, we encourage them to quickly find some kind of job to show that they have an attachment to the community. Finding an evening job may be a good idea, so that you're free during the day for job interviewing and informational interviewing. Another approach is to try to find a job with the company you want, regardless of what the job might be.

It's also important when moving to a new location to be realistic about where you are in your career and where you want to be. You might not be able to make that quantum leap; there might be a job or two jobs between your present position and your goal.

GOLDBERG: We've discussed several ways to look for a job: want ads, employment agencies, associations, networking, informational interviews, and college placement offices. Are there any other points you'd like to emphasize?

JOHNSON: Be prepared. Be prepared for rejection, because some people will not agree to an informational interview. Be prepared for disappointment, because what you discover in the informational interview might shatter a few of your preconceptions. The ability to bounce back from that rejection and disappointment is critical.

It's important to prepare for the informational interview by researching the company or employer. If I've agreed to meet with you for an informational interview, I would like to have the feeling when you get to my office that you know something about the field and something about the organization that I represent. I will be disappointed if you don't.

Finally, I would develop a laundry list of contacts, and I really do mean laundry list.

GOLDBERG: The message underlying everything else you've said seems to be: don't be passive as you go about the job hunt. You can begin of course with the want ads and employment agencies, but don't stop there. By becoming well informed about your options through contacts and networking and informational interviews, you have a good chance of selecting and being placed in a rewarding career.

CHAPTER 5

How to Make the
Interviewer Want You

You have to be bright and sensitive and you have to respond to the needs of the employer. You should display some energy, be loaded with information, and be as nice a person as you can be. Both of us should realize that we're on a blind date.

—Kirby Stanat

KIRBY STANAT'S career as a recruiter, placement officer, columnist, author, television host, and president of his own executive search firm is detailed in the introduction to Chapter Three. He is highly qualified to discuss the job interview, just as he is to discuss any other aspect of the job hunt.

GOLDBERG: We have come to the subject of the final process in landing a job: the interview. Before telling us how we can present ourselves well at an interview, would you share your thoughts about how we can get that interview appointment?

STANAT: First, instead of sending a resumé, you can simply call on companies that have advertised a job opening, or just walk in the front door. That's the least efficient way, but it's by far the most effective.

GOLDBERG: What happens if you walk into an office cold and ask to talk to the employer? I assume you'll meet some resistance.

STANAT: You can plan on spending a lot of time in the lobby, waiting for somebody to talk to you. While you're there, the only company you'll have will be the receptionist, and she will probably be trying to get rid of you. But receptionists don't hire, and the employment offer is never made in the lobby—it's made someplace back there in the bowels of the plant. So you have to get past that receptionist. And the most effective way to do that is to simply wait her out.

GOLDBERG: What would you say to her?

STANAT: My introduction would go something like this: "You had an ad in the paper for a production supervisor. I feel I'm qualified for that position and I'd like to speak to the individual who's making the hiring decision."

She'll probably say, "I'm sorry, that's Mr. Smith, and he only works by appointment." You can respond, "Fine, give me an appointment." If she suggests you leave your resumé, you can say, "I spent considerable effort getting here, hoping to meet with this gentleman, so if you don't mind, I'll simply wait until he's available."

Ordinarily, that person will see you, but it won't work every time. I know of instances when the receptionist said, "If you won't leave, I'll call the police." If that happens, leave! But ordinarily, if you've presented yourself in a reasonable fashion, she'll work in your behalf to get you in front of the individual who's doing the interviewing.

GOLDBERG: A lot of people reading this are probably saying to themselves, "Are you kidding? I can't walk in cold and say I want to see Mr. Smith. Only Clark Gable can pull that off."

STANAT: The only critical item in the whole employment process is the interview, and candidates should understand that getting the interview is *their* responsibility, not mine, as the employer or recruiter. I want to read your resumé—I can read six in a minute. I *don't* want to talk to you—I don't have enough time to do that. But since you'll never get a job without an interview, you *must* be aggressive, you must sit and wait, you must make cold calls. You must get out there and call on people. No interview: no job.

Also, remember that over 80 percent of the people in the nation work for companies that employ sixty or fewer people. These small employers depend on networking, on referrals, and on front-door traffic. You can identify those companies through the Yellow Pages and newspaper advertisements and call on them directly.

GOLDBERG: And if there's no job opening that you know of, if nothing's been advertised, what do you say?

STANAT: "Would you please direct me to the person in charge of hiring here. I need to talk with him."

GOLDBERG: "About what?"

STANAT: "About a job."

GOLDBERG: "We have no job openings advertised, sir."

STANAT: "Perhaps something will be coming up in the near future. In any case, I'd like to speak with this person so that a record of my interview can be on file."

GOLDBERG: If you succeed in seeing the person in charge of hiring, would that appointment become something like an informational interview?

STANAT: It could very well.

GOLDBERG: Why not use the tactic that Tom Johnson and Mary Kaupfer suggested? Instead of saying, "I'm here to get a job," say, "I'm here to learn about your company." That way you're less likely to meet resistance and more likely to get an interview.

STANAT: Either tactic could work. The important thing is that you sit down in front of the individual who makes the decision. And if I am interviewing you, I feel very strongly that you owe me four distinct things.

The first is that you must tell me what kind of position you're seeking. The individual who sits down and says, "I'm not real sure what I want to do," has forced the employer into the position of being a counselor. That's not my function, and I won't do it. Also, a lot of other things are communicated with that kind of uncertainty.

The second thing you must bring to the interview is some knowledge of me as the employer and what I do. What an insult it is for the candidate to say halfway through an interview, "Incidentally, what do you guys make?" The interview is over. That candidate is not seeking a career, but a job. There's a difference.

The third thing I need from the people I interview is that they be appropriately dressed. Go to that interview as if you're ready to go to work. If you're going to apply for a job on a shipping dock, you should be wearing clothes that are appropriate for the shipping dock. They should be neat and clean, but appropriate for the shipping dock. And if you're applying for a job as a receptionist, you should be ready to sit down as a receptionist. If the company to which you're applying is a public place, for instance a bank or a retail operation, it can be helpful to visit the day before and observe what employees are wearing.

The final thing I need from you is a sales pitch. For some reason, people in this country don't like to do that, don't like to sell themselves. The interview comes to an end and I ask, "Do you have any questions of me?" If you say, "No, I don't have any further questions," the interview is over. Other than the fact that you've shown up, you've not made a very strong statement of interest.

Here's the sales pitch: "From what I know of your organization, and what you've told me of the positions that may be available here, I'm really interested. I'd like to work here."

GOLDBERG: Let's go into each of these areas in depth, beginning with how we might prepare for an interview.

STANAT: I would research the employer as thoroughly as I could. That information is available in libraries, or from the chamber of commerce. If the stock is traded, it's available from brokers, and if nothing else, it's available from the employer.

If a company called me and said, "Would you come in at nine o'clock tomorrow for an interview?" I would say, "You bet. Can I come down this afternoon and pick up some information on your company?" I want to know their product line, how many offices they have, what services they perform, so that I can ask some intelligent questions in that interview and let them know that my interest in them is more than just superficial.

GOLDBERG: And when you sit down with this information and you start researching the company, what kinds of questions are you going to want to ask in the interview?

STANAT: There are all kinds of things: "I noticed that your sales went way up (or down) last year. Was there a particular reason for that?" Or, "I noticed that you opened four new offices in the past year. Do you plan to continue expanding?"

GOLDBERG: Are you asking those questions because you really care, or are you trying to make an impression of interest?

STANAT: Both.

GOLDBERG: But you can't lose by asking these kinds of questions?

STANAT: No, not at all.

GOLDBERG: You mentioned appearance as an important factor. Are there general guidelines that would apply if you were going to apply for a job as a sales executive in an insurance company, for example?

STANAT: A man should have on a white or a blue shirt, a quiet tie, lace-up shoes, and a blue or gray three-piece suit. A woman should be wearing low heels, a skirt, blouse, and blazer, or a suit.

GOLDBERG: Now suppose you're interviewing for a position as an account executive at an ad agency. How do you dress?

STANAT: If it's in Milwaukee, it's exactly the same way. If it's in Los Angeles, it's probably somewhat different. And if it's in Dallas, you can wear cowboy boots. There are certainly regional differences, but ordinarily, if you have any doubt, go the conservative route.

GOLDBERG: Why is it so important, at that corporate job, to have tied shoes rather than loafers?

STANAT: I don't know why it's so important, but it is. I talked to a young man recently who went to work for a Fortune 500 company as a field engineer. The opening statement from the vice-president in charge of his division was, "Sports coats do not exist." That doesn't make any sense to anybody, but it's the way things are, and people ought to know that.

GOLDBERG: What if you don't like to dress that way? What if you think you have lots of abilities, but one thing you don't want to do is wear a uniform every day to work?

STANAT: Too bad. If we're going to play in my sandbox with my trucks, we're going to play by my rules. Suppose I'm conducting a screening interview with you right now and you have a beard and a mustache. If I know that the manager in charge of that position hates beards and mustaches, I'm not going to take you down to see him. First, you're not going to get the job, and second, he's going to give me some heat.

GOLDBERG: But couldn't I make the argument that a beard and mustache could be a good screening device? If I would not be comfortable working with a manager who wouldn't like me for those reasons, or for a company with such formal standards, my beard and mustache might keep me from being misplaced.

STANAT: It also might keep you from an excellent opportunity. You might find out that other than this guy's idiotic mind set against beards and mustaches, he's a really nice guy and the company is doing some interesting work. You have to weigh all the factors.

GOLDBERG: If I interview with you for a job, how much will you learn about me during that minute or two before the interview really starts, as we introduce ourselves and sit down?

STANAT: A great deal. We'll both decide whether we have a chance of liking each other.

GOLDBERG: So there's a predisposition being set up right there.

STANAT: Yes.

GOLDBERG: What else will you learn in the interview?

STANAT: I already know you're qualified, although I'll make sure you've presented your qualifications accurately and that they're up to date. But what we're trying to do is to find out the things that you cannot put on paper. You won't tell me on a resumé how you smell, whether you wear too much cologne or an overpowering perfume. You can't put your smile on a resumé. And the interview is a chance to gauge your verbal skills and to see just how well you get along with other people.

GOLDBERG: What will we talk about in the interview?

STANAT: We'll talk about jobs. I'll ask you about what victories you've had, and what defeats. How did you handle the defeats? How did you work around them? I'll start to learn some things about you and your work habits and the way you define yourself in the workplace that cannot be described in a resumé.

GOLDBERG: How much do you value a person's professional background versus presence and likability?

STANAT: Most of what I'm searching for is whether or not I like an applicant. I have a number of employee evaluation check lists that are used by major employers. The word *qualifications* never appears on those check lists. Appearance is almost always the first item, and then communication skills, verbal skills, personality. These are the things that the final decision is based on. I can count on both hands the number of people I've hired that I've actively disliked. In every case, they had unusual qualifications in a very unusual skill area.

GOLDBERG: Is there a secret to being likable, to being the kind of person who would make an employer say, "I could work with this person."

STANAT: The secret is to be yourself. I don't think that you can go through any kind of significant personality shift and get away with it. I've already had forty-seven interviews this week and I'm pretty good at it. You're on your second one. You are junior varsity and I'm big league as far as experience in interviewing is concerned.

You're going to find most employers are pretty decent at making you feel comfortable. We know that this is a stressful situation for you and most of us are pretty good at putting you at ease. What you must do is be prepared to talk to me. I'm going to ask you questions you can't answer yes or no.

GOLDBERG: What are the questions that you can pretty well depend on being asked in any professional career interview?

STANAT: "Where do you want to be five years from now?" Or, "What are your goals?" If you've had professional experience, I would ask, "What have been your victories and your defeats on the job?" I may ask, "What do you perceive as your most significant strengths? And what do you perceive as your most significant weaknesses?"

GOLDBERG: How would you answer that last question?

STANAT: You turn your weaknesses into pluses. "My most significant weakness is that I have a tendency to work too hard."

GOLDBERG: And they'll say, "Mr. Stanat, is that your only weakness?"

STANAT: "No, it's not my only weakness. I don't do well with detail; I'm more of a conceptual person. If you want a magnificent team, you might pair me with someone who's very interested in detail."

GOLDBERG: Should you list all of your weaknesses or just the ones you think won't hurt your chances of being hired?

STANAT: If you put me in a job that I don't like or can't handle very well, nobody's going to come out ahead, and I may even lose the job. Then I'll have a problem on my resumé that I didn't have before.

If I can't handle detail, if it drives me nuts, I probably ought to tell somebody about that, and it should be kept in mind when I'm being placed within the organization.

GOLDBERG: Will an employer like you more for being honest about weaknesses?

STANAT: Yes. A wonderful thing that often happens in the employment process is that as you and I start talking, we truly develop an appreciation for each other. I might switch you into another job, one that you didn't even apply for. I might say, "The job you applied for isn't for you, but there are a couple of other openings that I haven't told anybody about yet. How does this one sound?"

And often I get myself into a situation where I feel very comfortable about making a compromise—and every job placement is a compromise. I've never hired the perfect individual. There's always been a compromise about age or money or educational level or something like that. And if I really like who I'm seeing, I'll take the chance of walking down the hall and saying, "Hey, Mr. Manager, this guy doesn't quite fit, but we've got a lot to work with."

GOLDBERG: What questions should the candidate ask the employer during the interview?

STANAT: You can take a lot of the questions that the recruiter has asked you and turn them around so that they work in your behalf. He or she may ask you, "Where do you want to be in five years?" You'll answer that question, but then it's very fair to ask in return, "If I'm a good solid employee, where *am* I going to be in five years?" One way or another, you can and should ask what growth opportunities are available.

GOLDBERG: Should you ask about salary and benefits and vacations?

STANAT: I don't think that happens until the last half of the ninth inning, and ordinarily questions about fringes don't have to be asked, because if you've picked up the appropriate information about the company, you'll already have the answers. You should be very careful that you don't ask questions that are included in the company information, because that tells me something.

GOLDBERG: Some people have skeletons in their closet: they've been fired from a job, or been to jail, or have a serious health problem. How do you handle those issues in the interview?

STANAT: I suggest you avoid those skeletons until we get to the actual job offer. At that point you say, "I didn't include this in the previous conversation because I thought it would be counterproductive. I want you to know that I'm a severe diabetic. It's been under control and I don't have a lot of problems with it, but I thought you should know about it."

GOLDBERG: Will that blow the job right there and then?

STANAT: It might, but we're going to have to deal with it sooner or later. Do keep it as far back in the process as you can.

GOLDBERG: Is that because the employer is already sold on you at this point?

STANAT: Yes.

GOLDBERG: The interview's coming to an end. Mr. Smith says, "Well, thanks very much for coming in. We'll be in touch with you." Now what do you do?

STANAT: You never leave the ball in his court. You ask when you can expect to hear from him. If you don't hear from him then, you wait one working day and then call him and say, "Maybe I misunderstood, but I was expecting to hear from you yesterday. I continue to be very interested in the position. Do you need further information?"

GOLDBERG: Do you ever call before Mr. Smith said he was going to call you—the next day, for instance—to say, "I really want this job."

STANAT: No, not unless you have some problems and the problems are good ones. You can certainly call to say, "I've received another job offer, but I'm really more interested in your job. Can you possibly move your decision date up a little bit?"

GOLDBERG: Any final words as you're saying good-bye?

STANAT: Go back to the sales pitch: "From what I know of this company and what I know of the position after talking to you today, I would really like to work here. I hope you consider me a serious candidate."

GOLDBERG: How do you sell yourself throughout the interview?

STANAT: You have to be bright and sensitive and you have to be responsive to the needs of the employer. You should display some energy, be loaded with information, and be as nice a person as you can. Both of us should realize that we're on a blind date.

The first thing I may say to you is, "Would you like to have a cup of coffee?" And I ask my secretary to go and get you a cup of coffee. But after today, Buster, go and get your own coffee. I mean, we're in a false environment, and we both know that. We're both on our very best behavior.

GOLDBERG: Is it accurate to look at this as primarily a passive experience on the part of the candidate?

STANAT: Very much so. And the only time you should jump in and take control is when you're asked if you have any questions. That's your opportunity to ask about the company and about issues that would concern you in the job. Other than that, you should respond crisply and efficiently and try to sense how much information the employer needs.

GOLDBERG: Let me review some of the ground we've covered. You've said that the importance of dressing for the job cannot be overestimated and that it's appropriate to dress at the interview as you would dress for the job. It is also essential to prepare for the interview by learning something about the employer. During the interview, be yourself. If the employer doesn't like who you are, it's in everybody's best interest to find that out up front. Finally, make a sales pitch at the end of the interview; let the employer know you're enthusiastic about the position.

CHAPTER 6

Special Issues of the Returning Homemaker

> I see a total turnaround in the way women value themselves. When a woman's been in the home, she may not have felt fulfilled or she may not have had a lot of contact with other people. Suddenly she's in a whole different environment. She's feeling competent and assertive and she's having dialogues with other people who interest her. All different kinds of things are happening to her that make her life new and exciting and challenging.
> —*Samantha River*

LISA MUNRO and SAMANTHA RIVER have both met plenty of homemakers who have been in the process of returning to the workplace, but they've met them in different capacities. A returning homemaker exploring vocational directions or the options that further education might give her is likely to run into Lisa at the University of Wisconsin's Continuing Educational Services Department. If that same homemaker is interested in finding out about jobs that are immediately available or if she is seeking vocational counseling, she might well talk with Samantha, who is the executive director at Skilled Jobs for Women in Madison.

GOLDBERG: The growing population in the work force is women. In fact, the work force is approximately 50 percent female at this point, and the percentage continues to grow. Many of the women who are entering or reentering the work force now are older than their early twenties, and many have devoted years to their homes and families. Of this group, a large number have college degrees, and they are concerned that now, five or ten or twenty years after that degree was granted, it might have lost some of its value in the jobs marketplace. In fact, the returning homemaker often has many questions about the value of her education, her skills, and her background when it comes to the world of work.

We are going to address the issues that those women face, issues that are substantially different from those of the recent college graduate or the career switcher.

How is the working environment different for women today than it was in the early seventies?

RIVER. There's a much greater acceptance of women in the labor market and many more options in terms of different types of careers. Nontraditional jobs have opened up tremendously for women, both blue collar and professional. Many jobs are more available to women due to affirmative action, including jobs in fields that they might not have been able to consider back in the seventies.

Also, because so many women are in the work force, instead of the isolation that they might have felt in the early seventies if they had gone into professional fields, they'll now find that many of their colleagues are women.

MUNRO: Women feel different about being back in the work force and continuing to be part-time homemakers. They feel less guilty about working while they raise children than they did in the seventies, and certainly than they did in the fifties and sixties.

RIVER: There's a lot more flexibility in the work force, too. Things like job sharing and half-time work are becoming national trends now, so that often a mother who has younger children and wants to be home in the afternoon after school can do that. Generally, there are many · more options for working women than there used to be. In the seventies, you worked your job from eight to four-thirty or nine to five, or you probably didn't work. That's not true anymore.

GOLDBERG: You mentioned nontraditional jobs. What kinds of jobs are nontraditional for women?

RIVER: Anything that you would normally have expected a man to do. A lot of women are going through apprenticeship programs and getting journeymen's cards in the construction trades: painting, plumbing, bricklaying—things like that. Women who have been in the home may have been doing the painting or fixing the broken toaster, and they may have found that they have an aptitude for some of those things.

GOLDBERG: Do you see women with college degrees in these nontraditional fields?

RIVER: With an amazing frequency. A lot of women returning to the work force choose not to work in an environment that they had chosen to work in before. They may have learned that they do not want to sit behind a desk, and that they want to be able to use their hands and use their bodies.

Nontraditional can also comprise the professional trades—law, for example, or medicine or accounting. About a third of most graduating law classes now are female.

GOLDBERG: Let's say you have to make a bet. You're counseling two women with comparable skills, both with humanities degrees. One is twenty-two years old and just getting out of college. The other is thirty-six years old and is a returning homemaker. Which woman is going to get a good job faster?

MUNRO: I would be concerned about the older woman's level of self-confidence—it's one of the most critical elements that women returning to the work force have to struggle with. Usually people in their early twenties have loads of self-confidence; they're optimistic and excited about experiencing what the world has to offer.

GOLDBERG: They're too young to know what they don't know yet?

MUNRO: Correct. But the housewife has had a few bruises over economic and relationship issues, and has seen that some of her dreams have not turned out as expected. She may be less confident and optimistic.

RIVER: Still, it's likely that the woman who's reentering the work force has worked before, so her resumé will show a work history, even if it's not recent. And a lot depends on the employer, of course, and what he or she is looking for. Maturity is one of the things that a homemaker has always got to sell, assuming her self-confidence is at a level where she can sell herself. That's often *the* big issue for a returning homemaker.

GOLDBERG: How do you begin to approach issues of assertiveness and worthiness when you're talking with a homemaker who is entering the work force?

MUNRO: First, you have to spend some time with a woman to get a sense of her own self-assessment. Usually the women I see who are considering returning to the work force haven't had much opportunity to develop or clarify goals, or even to make major life decisions. So it's useful to start developing these areas.

GOLDBERG: Isn't that a contradiction? You said that homemaking involves many skills and responsibilities, but you now say that most homemakers haven't made major decisions or experienced the kinds of responsibilities that would give them a basis of self-confidence.

MUNRO: The problem is a combination of our society devaluing the homemaker role, the fact that it's not a paid profession, and the fact that it's not generally recognized as a role that takes special skills. In reality, it does take skill to do it well.

GOLDBERG: What kinds of skills?

MUNRO: Communication skills, public relations skills, management skills. Even with only one child, juggling schedules can get complicated. If your family is larger, you need to have excellent organizational skills. Many women handle all the budgets for their family and they are much more knowledgeable and astute about the family financial situation than their husband. Women are often the mechanical wizards in the family. There are a lot of myths about what the man does versus what the woman does.

RIVER: Find out who really paints the closets—it's almost always the woman. Women are chauffeurs and nurses; they do the laundry, they cook, they shop. We're dealing with a cultural frame of mind that says, "Anybody can do that stuff." That's not true. To do it and do it fairly well, you have to have learned a group of skills.

I once sat down with some colleagues and figured out how many trades it takes to be a successful homemaker. It takes about thirty-two. And a newspaper article I read recently stated that if we had to pay homemakers for what they do—for the same services provided outside the home—they'd average about $40,000 a year. So we've got to get the homemaker to realize that there's no such thing as "just a homemaker."

Now, some women are terrible homemakers—you have to say that too. They don't do any of it very well, but perhaps they gain some skills by trying.

GOLDBERG: What can you say about the ones who are terrible homemakers?

RIVER: They do better in jobs! They're often very competent in the work force, and very happy, because what made them terrible homemakers is that they didn't like themselves in that role. Trying to carry on an intelligent conversation with a two-year-old can be boring. Hanging out at the grocery store day after day can get dull. For many women, it's a great relief to go to work and deal with adults and the kinds of challenges that a job brings.

GOLDBERG: We were just examining the functions of a homemaker and isolating skills as they might relate to a professional career. Is it useful for a homemaker to make that kind of an evaluation if she's planning to look for a job?

MUNRO: Yes. This kind of assessment is something that anyone could do in making career decisions. It includes assessing skills, analyzing interests and background, and determining values. By values I mean the rewards one wants for one's work—both nonmonetary and monetary rewards.

RIVER: A good counseling or employment service can identity aptitudes, skills, interests, and abilities and basically match them to jobs.

GOLDBERG: Where can homemakers find that kind of help? Do they open the Yellow Pages to "counseling"?

MUNRO: Many colleges and universities have a Continuing Education Office or Returning Women's Center—some kind of counseling service. Thousands of women are returning to school and to the labor force, and because education and employment are so intertwined, universities and colleges realize the need for this kind of service.

GOLDBERG: Once a homemaker has assessed her skills and interest, she may still need help in coping with low morale. How can she overcome her sense that she's not good enough, or her feelings of selfishness at thinking of herself first after years of nurturing her family?

MUNRO: There are many groups for returning homemakers that focus on exactly these issues. "Women in transition" is a term often used to identify groups or workshops based on this theme. Usually, once women get together with other women and recognize that they aren't alone in their feelings, they can start to develop some assertiveness skills. And it does take some new learning. Many of these women were raised at a time when being a traditional female was highly valued. They've deferred to their husbands in most decision making. They're used to a passive role. These women are going to have to learn some new approaches.

RIVER: At Skilled Jobs for Women, we have a support group that meets regularly for women who are what we call "displaced home-makers." They get together and find out the same things that you just mentioned, that there's a great mutuality. They begin to see the patterns that they have all developed and they realize that some of these patterns are not valid. Once they come to that realization, they are ready to market themselves. They have the confidence to say, "I might have felt this way, but it's probably just because I was isolated."

GOLDBERG: You mentioned displaced homemakers. As I under-stand it, those are women who are thrust into the job market through divorce or the death of their spouse. What special issues does the displaced homemaker face?

RIVER: She may be a woman who never planned to go back to work, who was content with her role as a housewife and thought that that was what she'd be doing for the rest of her life. Suddenly, she is in a position where she has to go back to work to support her-self, and often her children, too. If her husband is disabled, she may have to support him as well.

She has to deal with all the issues we've already discussed, plus she'll generally have a lot of anger about the position she finds her-self in. Often she has a very hard time with the basic fact that she's got to go to work. It's common for a displaced homemaker to go into an interview and say, "I'd really like to work here, but every Thurs-day I have to be off because Johnny goes to baseball, and at 4:30 on Tuesdays my daughter goes to the orthodontist, so I'll need that time off." Her priorities are obviously at home. She'll have to shift those priorities to accommodate both the home and the job.

GOLDBERG: Why would a boss hire someone who's halfhearted about coming to work, who leaves the impression that the career isn't that important, that home is a higher priority? Why hire that person when someone else wants to work for you who is really ex-cited and enthusiastic?

MUNRO: Before she starts the interviewing process, the home-maker should take the time to assess the importance of work for her, otherwise she'll be doing a disservice to the employer and to herself. If she comes to the interview still having major questions about her desire to work, she will sabotage herself and the employer will not hire her.

GOLDBERG: Let's talk about that whole hiring process: writing the resumé, finding the job opening, landing the interview. It all begins, I presume, with the resumé. In what way is a resumé different for the returning homemaker than for everyone else?

RIVER: There's likely to be a big hole in the resumé, which represents her homemaking years. She has to come up with some tangible way to show what was in that hole. Instead of using a chronological resumé—which says, "In 1979, I did this; in 1980, I did this"—she can write a functional resumé, which allows her to list her skills and abilities and elaborate on experiences that bear on those skills and abilities.

MUNRO: One advantage of a functional resumé is that once a woman starts working on it, she'll start to realize the number of skills she has. All kinds of legitimate skills are hidden in volunteer work and hobbies, as well as in homemaking activities. This realization can enhance her self-confidence immensely.

GOLDBERG: What about looking for the job openings? Want ads only represent a very small percentage of the job market. How else can the returning homemaker find the available positions?

MUNRO: Anyone who has worked with career issues is familiar with what we call the hidden job market, the many positions that are never put out into any public record. Finding those requires an assertive hunt, making contact with many different kinds of people who can direct you to other people or who have information about what jobs are opening up, what companies are looking at new directions, etc. So we're talking about an active job hunt, where you are creatively and energetically trying to follow up on lots of different personal leads.

GOLDBERG: Are networking and informational interviewing any different for the returning homemaker than anyone else?

RIVER: The returning homemaker probably has a different network than does a person who's been in the job market. If you've been in the job market and you want to keep working in the same field, you have the advantage of knowing where to go, who to talk to, who might be hiring, who might be getting more money—that sort of thing.

If you're a homemaker, you've got a whole other network that you may not even realize you have. If you've been doing volunteer work, you've got the people that you're working with and their spouses and families. If you belong to a church, you can network there. I generally say to people at this point, start seeing through the see-through walls. As you drive down the street, think,"Who makes that building work? What's in there that I could do?" And you need to start thinking of people in different ways. Instead of thinking, "Good old Joe. I should invite him to a party," you think, "Joe runs his own business. He hires forty-five people a year. I should talk to him."

Also, nobody's in a better position than a homemaker to do a community-needs assessment. She's the one who knows if there's no day care in her area or no Stop 'n' Go on her corner. She'll know if there's no secondhand clothing store within twenty miles. She has better access to that information than anybody else around.

GOLDBERG: What does she do with that information?

RIVER: She can turn it into a real marketable job for herself. If she knows that you've got to go twenty miles to get to a used clothing store and all of her friends are going over there every three days, she might decide to open one down the street. Then she's got her own business, and since she has identified a community need, she has a good chance of success.

GOLDBERG: And because the homemaker does the books, does the repairs around the house, has interpersonal skills, she might be very well equipped to open her own small business.

RIVER: It also has advantages in terms of combining her career with her home life. If you're the boss, you can decide when you want to go on vacation or what hours you'll work. You have much more flexibility than when plugging into an established structure.

GOLDBERG: Are there other advantages in networking and locating job openings that a forty-five-year-old returning homemaker might have over a twenty-three-year-old who has just gotten her degree?

MUNRO: There are a lot of advantages just in terms of time. The older woman has been there in her community, getting to know it well and making contacts. She's earned a certain number of good-will points in terms of social interaction with lots of different kinds of people. She may be able to reach people at higher levels than the twenty-three-year-old, because she's run into those people during the course of ordinary social contact. And often people are very willing to assist someone just because they know who they are and have enjoyed their company. They'll go that extra mile for them. It's unlikely that the twenty-three-year-old will have that kind of advantage.

These contacts are the homemaker's resources and she needs to value them and use them to her own advantage. The question is whether she has the assertiveness to do that.

GOLDBERG: Let's move to the job interview and imagine a tough situation. Suppose an employer says, "Well, Barbara, you've spent thirteen years chauffeuring kids around, being a homemaker. If you're that interested in writing ad copy, why have you kept yourself out of it all that time?" How does she answer?

MUNRO: She can explain that part of her philosophy of work is that she wants to do a very competent job in whatever she's engaged in. For that period of time she was interested in providing as good a home environment for her children as possible. Her children are now in a position where they don't need her as much and she's ready for a different kind of environment.

RIVER: She should be able to reach in her purse and pull out the program she did for the senior play—or a flyer for a raffle or a poster for a school fair. Sometimes a homemaker can put together a whole portfolio of things she's done through volunteering or hobbies.

MUNRO: One obstacle that can come up in the interview and that needs to be realistically dealt with is the age factor. I'm seeing more and more older women interested in returning to the work force. These might be people whose children are grown and out of the home. I don't want to underestimate the difficulty of the age issue.

GOLDBERG: How old are you talking about?

MUNRO: Mid-forties.

GOLDBERG: And are you saying it is more difficult the longer you've been away from the market?

MUNRO: I don't think that's the issue. It's not being away from the market, it's the age factor. Even executives who have lost positions because their companies have been bought out are running into some problems.

RIVER: The older applicant may have some difficulty convincing an employer that she'll be there. There are a lot of myths about absenteeism—"she's not going to drive in the snow," for example.

MUNRO: My feeling is that the older homemaker should probably bring up the age issue herself. She might say, "You may be concerned about the fact that I am in my mid-forties. I don't see that as being an obstacle. On the contrary, I think my years of experience and the kinds of wisdom I have gained would make me an asset. I am mature and I am conscientious. A younger person might be interested in moving up the ladder quickly and leaving town, going where the better opportunities are. I have roots in the community and plan to remain here."

GOLDBERG: Any other tips about preparing for the interview?

MUNRO: I suggest writing out answers to specific questions and possibly using a tape recorder to record and listen to your answers. Real professional work ahead of time will pay off.

GOLDBERG: Suppose the interviewer asks whether you're planning to have more children?

RIVER: Technically, that is not a question that employers are supposed to ask. You can even take them to court over it, but generally that is not the best way to get a job. You might say, "At this point in my life, I do not foresee having any more children."

GOLDBERG: What if you *do* plan to have other children?

MUNRO: Most employers who have any women working in their organization have dealt with maternity leave. I don't think they see it as being that much of an obstacle.

GOLDBERG: Of the returning homemakers you see who have a bachelor's or graduate degree, who needs to and who doesn't need to go back to school and get retooled?

MUNRO: The person who needs retooling is the person who has decided she wants to go into an area that requires specific, specialized knowledge. Certainly this includes some of the high-tech careers that we're hearing so much about in engineering and data processing and material science and robotics.

RIVER: Another thing we're seeing right now is a tremendous surge in people entering the service occupations: managing restaurants, child care, and so on. These are jobs that a homemaker is likely to have a good background in because they use many of the same skills that she's been using in the home. They are jobs that she could definitely consider doing without going back and getting retooling.

Other than technical stuff, this is probably where a majority of the jobs are now. We're moving from being an industrial economy into becoming more of a service economy, and so the homemaker is actually in a good position to market her skills.

GOLDBERG: What are the most difficult problems for the home-maker returning to the work force?

MUNRO: She has to constantly juggle a lot of different demands. It can be exhausting.

RIVER: How do you get somebody to fill in the gaps that are left when there's no homemaker in the house? How do you deal with the stress? Often women feel guilty about leaving their children. And do they pay half their salary out in day care? Do they have latch-key kids who let themselves in after school and baby-sit for themselves until five o'clock, when somebody comes home?

You've got to balance all that stuff, and I'd say the worst thing is stress, just a whole lot of stress about all the different things that you're expecting yourself to do, and do competently. You've got to come up with some compromises—maybe change the sheets only every two weeks or eat at McDonald's every so often. You can't be supermother and a great professional career person and all those other things at a level of total competence. You've got to give your-self some slack.

MUNRO: Some returning homemakers run into problems in terms of dealing with their family's lack of support. There's a lot of eco-nomic pressure for women to return to the work force, but there may be negative feelings about it from the husband and children or the in-laws and parents. And sometimes women feel guilty about the excitement that they feel in being able to leave the home and do something else.

GOLDBERG: Suppose a husband says, "I don't want you to get a job. I want you here." And his wife says, "Well, our kids are old enough not to need me here all the time." And he says, "I don't care. I don't want you to get a job." How can the wife deal with that?

MUNRO: I would encourage her to assess how strongly her interest is in returning to the work force, and assuming that it's high, she's going to have to try to work at reeducating her husband. Maybe she can help change his feelings about his role in the home and his role as her husband, and she can help him become more supportive and feel less threatened about her returning to work.

GOLDBERG: I think you're putting it gently. There are going to be a lot of fights.

MUNRO: There can be some real strains in the marriage.

RIVER: I would encourage this woman to try to break her hus-band in gradually, perhaps starting with a job that only requires her to work quarter-time. There's generally a way to ease into it if you're getting a lot of tension at home.

GOLDBERG: I can imagine some women feeling, "But he's wrong! I deserve the right to work if I want to and if I don't need to be in the home. I don't have to assuage his male ego."

RIVER: That woman's in trouble. She has to decide what's most important to her. Is she willing to deal with the fallout of saying, "I don't care what you think. I'm going to work"? If so, then that's what she should do.

MUNRO: If we carry that a few steps farther, it brings up another issue. A homemaker who is successful in the workplace and is moving up in the organization may find that she is going to have to wrestle with certain demands the company may put on her. Usually that means time. Men traditionally have been able to travel or put in a lot of overtime because the wife picks up the slack. But what happens in this situation? If she still has young children and wants to continue to put a certain amount of her time and energy into the home, there may have to be some reorganizing of family roles and a continuing assessment of values.

RIVER: Probably most devastating of all is when a wife returns to the work force and within a few years equals or exceeds her husband's salary. He begins to question his value and then problems really arise.

GOLDBERG: For the returning homemaker going into a job, what will be the best part of the experience?

MUNRO: From reports I've read, they generally feel much more fulfilled and excited about their lives. I have seen evidence that women who are living multiple roles tend to feel that they enjoy life more. They find that being a parent, a spouse, and a working person taps into different parts of their personality and their skills and they feel better about how they're living their lives.

RIVER: I see a total turnaround in the way that the woman values herself. When she was in the home, she may not have felt fulfilled or she may not have had a lot of contact with other people. Suddenly she's in a whole new environment. She's feeling competent and assertive and she's having dialogues with other people who interest her. All kinds of things are happening to her that make her life new and exciting and challenging. ·

GOLDBERG: Let me sum up some of what we've talked about. On the whole, the eighties is a pretty good time for the homemaker to return to the job market, considering the number and variety of jobs that are available. Many skills gained in homemaking can be applied to jobs, but the returning homemaker has to learn to present those skills with pride. She also has to learn to believe in her right to have a career, although she may have to weigh her desire for a job against family resistance. The returning homemaker doesn't have to be retooled unless she wants a career that's in a specialized area such as computer science. She can use her social contacts as legitimate resources as she looks for job openings. The one big stumbling block for the returning homemaker is her lack of self-confidence.

CHAPTER 7

Successful Career Switching

Most of all, you're selling yourself. That's a cliché, but it's all the more true in a career-switching situation. You don't have specific skills and training to offer, so above all else you're selling your potential.

—Leslie Goldsmith

LESLIE GOLDSMITH and CYNTHIA KABAT meet frequently with men and women who are considering changing their careers, and they are fully aware of the stresses it can cause for both the career switcher and his or her family. Cynthia is a vocational counselor and an employment coordinator for Skilled Jobs for Women, where, among other assignments, she leads workshops about career changes. Leslie is an independent career counselor and the director of a publicly funded employment agency.

GOLDBERG: How often do people switch careers?

KABAT: The average is three to four switches in a lifetime. Of course, there's a myth that people plug into jobs for twenty-five or thirty years and then retire. The truth is that up to 20 percent of the entire working population is out of work in a given year, thinking about switching careers, and about 40 million Americans are in some stage of career transition right now.

GOLDBERG: Forty million out of about 100 million in the work force?

KABAT: That's right. And another statistic shows that 80 percent of working people are underemployed, working in jobs that are not making use of their skills. That can result in frustration and boredom and the desire to switch.

GOLDBERG: Whose fault is that?

KABAT: It has to do partly with what jobs are available, and partly with the fact that people are not trained to look at their skills and go for jobs that utilize their strengths. They go instead for what's easy. Also, because of shifts in the job market and the population trends, we have more people in the work force than ever before. We don't have enough jobs to go around at the level at which everyone wants to work.

GOLDBERG: By switches, do we mean, for instance, a person who is working in a bank and moves to another bank in the same position, but with a little higher salary?

KABAT: The term really means a change to a different position. The person may be in the same company, but the job has actually changed.

GOLDSMITH: I've heard that the average American worker switches jobs, not necessarily careers, every three to four years. That's a lot of mobility and it's partly due to the structural changes in the labor market. For example, I trained for a field in which there were no jobs. The fact that I liked what I was doing didn't help. Many people don't give much thought to what they want to do, and they train for situations that they find out are not very satisfying. Other people switch for financial reasons or because they relocate.

GOLDBERG: I've heard figures different from what both of you are presenting. I've heard career counselors say that people switch careers five or six times in a lifetime. So I guess different sources quote different figures, but the consensus is that people switch a lot.

KABAT: And it's increasing. That's why you're seeing the difference in statistics. And younger people are switching more frequently than older.

GOLDBERG: Why?

KABAT: The baby boom generation is making a bulge in the work force; and the reality is that they can't *all* move up. So they start moving laterally, which means a career switch.

GOLDBERG: When people switch from one career to another, what are their motives?

GOLDSMITH: Most people change because they're dissatisfied with either their job or their level of pay, and I meet lots of people who are willing to sacrifice pay to do something more satisfying. And as more and more people around them change careers they feel more and more justified in considering it as an option for themselves.

GOLDBERG: Why do so many people find their jobs dissatisfying?

GOLDSMITH: First, there is no way to accurately predict whether you will like something unless you try it. Also, individuals are dynamic, changing forces. Just because something is right for you now doesn't mean that it's going to be right for you five or ten years from now. And life circumstances change, the world changes around us.

GOLDBERG: Is it the human condition to get bored with what you're doing, no matter what it is, after a certain period of time?

GOLDSMITH: I think so. Most people at least get into a routine, and for many people that can be defined as boredom. The older generation grew up in a different era. Many of them started working at a time when a job—any job—was *the* most valued thing. They didn't have the option of switching careers. Also, during the postwar era jobs became too lucrative for some to think about switching. That's not necessarily the case anymore.

GOLDBERG: When do you know that you're getting the itch? What are the signs that you're about to make a jump?

GOLDSMITH: You start screwing up on the job, not wanting to do your assignments, procrastinating. You have a general malaise and feeling of dissatisfaction. You sleep late, miss work for various reasons. A lot of these things become tied up with what psychologists would call clinical depression, although it's usually not that serious.

GOLDBERG: What's going on in your mind if you're becoming dissatisfied with a professional career that you had prepared for and perhaps gotten a degree or two to qualify for?

KABAT: A lot of internalization. "What's wrong with me? Why can't I stay with this? I prepared for this: I should like it." A lot of "should" messages.

GOLDSMITH: A lot of guilt about feeling this way. And the most helpful thing at this point is to seek out other people who are feeling the same way or who have already changed careers, so that you don't feel so isolated.

KABAT: I tell people in this situation that their feelings are normal, and however they handle the situation is normal. It's frustrating and depressing at first, but eventually you get beyond that into the exploration of new options for your life. If you realize that, you can start changing the anger and frustration into excitement.

GOLDBERG: Does the word *rebirth* strike you as appropriate?

KABAT: For many, that's how it feels. Whenever you take depression and unfocused energy and you find a goal or a direction, the feeling is exhilaration.

GOLDBERG: Let's talk about the steps, the how-to's. Where do you begin the process of the career switch?

KABAT: You have to find small ways to start exploring. Talk to other people who have made career switches, talk with individuals who are doing something you think you might want to do. That's referred to as informational interviewing and it's an easy thing to do. You can do it on a lunch break or another break. In some cases, you can do it while you're working.

GOLDSMITH: You need to identify what it is about your present career and things you've done in the past that you do and do not like. It's easier to talk this through with someone and it doesn't need to be a professional counselor. It can help to bounce ideas around with a friend or an acquaintance—anyone who will give you some objective guidance. If you're working by yourself, you can get in a rut and it can be hard to identify what it is about yourself or your situation that's problematic.

GOLDBERG: I'd like to play the role of someone who's in the throes of what we've been talking about.

This is my problem: I got my master's in social work and have been a social worker, listening to people's problems, for nine years now. But I'm just burned out. I'm making $16,000 a year, working at a mental health agency. The pay's not going to get much better—maybe in five years I'll make $19,000. And I don't know what to do. I don't know where to begin.

GOLDSMITH: I wonder whether you're dissatisfied with your present situation or with your entire career. Try to go back and identify the reasons that you went into social work to begin with. Are those reasons still valid?

GOLDBERG: I went into it because I like people. I like feeling helpful, and to be honest, there's a little piece of me that likes to peek into people's lives. I've always been interested in what makes people tick.

KABAT: Are those things that you're still interested in?

GOLDBERG: I'm finding that my interests are shifting. I'm not interested anymore in working so hard to solve other people's problems, and I'm also finding out that it's very hard to help people change. I'm interested, but not with the same commitment I had a few years ago.

GOLDSMITH: Do you have any fantasies about other jobs, other things you'd like to do?

GOLDBERG: I'd like a lot of money. By a lot, I don't mean millions, but $25–30,000 a year. I have a wife who works, and we're talking about having kids. I'd have to make more money.

GOLDSMITH: If you weren't a social worker, what would you like to be?

GOLDBERG: That's a hard question. I don't know if I can answer it directly. I'd like to be just a little more removed from people and a little more in the business mainstream. I don't like the idea of getting dressed up in a suit every day, but I like the idea of some of the things that people in suits do.

One thing that does intrigue me is investments. I find myself reading about investments, stocks, gold, and all that stuff, and I really find it interesting. I'm surprised I do, but I do. We don't have a lot of savings, but I've bought some stocks and I get a kick out of it. And I've made a little money.

GOLDSMITH: Have you ever talked to an investment counselor?

GOLDBERG: No, I haven't.

KABAT: That might be a good next step. You can see how that profession combines your old interest of working with people with your new interest in investments. Take a look at the work, what the environment's like, the social interaction. See if you feel comfortable in that setting.

GOLDSMITH: If you find that it does intrigue you, then it would be time to put together a resumé, go back to some of the people you talked to for informational purposes, tell them you've decided that this is the career you want. Seek other contacts, form a network in one way or another, and interview for some jobs.

GOLDBERG: When you counsel career changers, do you find it very taxing?

GOLDSMITH: The most difficult thing for me is helping them arrive at suitable alternatives. That can sometimes be a very laborious process. It's taxing for me, and for the client, to weed through what he or she does or doesn't like about the current job, life-style, etc. But I emphasize *alternatives* in the plural, because what you have to do is come up with several different approaches and send the client out on several different paths; if one doesn't pan out, maybe another one will.

GOLDBERG: Do you think it's better for people to quit their job to make this search, or stay in their job?

KABAT: It depends on the individual. I ask them, "How much risk can you tolerate? How many financial debts do you have? Do you have a family? Will you have to have a certain amount of money coming in if you're not working? Have you been through a lot of stress in the recent past, so that another major stress might cause illness? Or are you the kind of person whose style it is to go for it, so that the only way you're ever going to make a change is to leave what you're doing and go full force?"

GOLDBERG: Is it a full-time job to search for another job?

KABAT: Basically. You have to be out there making contacts, being available.

GOLDBERG: Then how can you do it if you don't quit your present job?

KABAT: By changing your timeline. By putting in however much time you can and realizing that it's going to take you longer.

GOLDBERG: Are you less desirable in the eyes of the employer if you quit your job and are unemployed while looking for another job?

GOLDSMITH: With some exceptions, I think you are. Many employers, perhaps unconsciously, classify an unemployed person as a loser.

GOLDBERG: If the shift is dramatic, say if you're going from social work to selling investments, wouldn't it matter less? Does the stockbroker's firm really care if you're a social worker in practice or a former social worker?

KABAT: My guess is that when you have a drastic change from one career to another, they'll be more receptive to your being unemployed.

GOLDBERG: So we're at a middle ground. If your switch is only sidestepping, that is, only a small change from the type of career you're in, then you're more likely to be hurt by quitting than if it's a radical change.

GOLDSMITH: I'm not sure you can generalize to that extent. It's going to be different for each person in each situation.

KABAT: It's one of those basic career issues, where two things are true at the same time, and there's really no way to resolve it. Many employers out there are under the impression that people should not leave jobs. Others are sensitive to the fact that if you want to get ahead, you might have to leave.

GOLDBERG: Once you've figured out the kind of new career you want, is the next step to write a resumé or look for a job? Which comes first?

KABAT: At our agency, one of the first things we have clients do, before writing a resumé or arranging interviews, is look at what could prevent them from succeeding. They've made a career decision, now we look at what barriers might arise. They need to look at questions like these: is there going to be a financial problem? If so, how can it be resolved? Will there be stress on the family? Will somebody be switching roles? Who is going to take up what duty? Are they still feeling some depression? Do they need to develop more assertiveness? More verbal skills?

GOLDBERG: How about the resumé? Are there special issues here for the career switcher?

KABAT: Because they're switching careers, they won't want to emphasize the specific places they've worked, or their specific job titles. Those aren't relevant. Instead, they have to look into their former employment and see how they can describe it so that it's relevant to a new employer. And they can emphasize their skills— interpersonal skills, organizational skills, financial investment skills, and so on. In this way they form what we call a "skill base."

GOLDBERG: Let's go back to the guy who was a social worker for nine years and now wants to become a stockbroker. How would he write his resumé?

GOLDSMITH: In his case, investing has been a hobby, and I'd put that right up on top in terms of desirable qualifications. It's almost incidental that he was a social worker for nine years, although if there are portions of that job that dealt with fiscal matters, those should also be moved to the top of the resumé. Anything that relates to your job objectives should be put right up front, so that the employer can immediately make the connection and understand why this resumé of a social worker has suddenly appeared on his desk.

KABAT: He can also emphasize his skills in communicating with people, being able to interview people and discuss their problems. That's what brokers do. If you know what the career area you're going into requires, you can look at your background and find what in it qualifies you.

GOLDBERG: Any special tips for career switchers when it comes to finding job openings?

KABAT: Something like 75 percent of all jobs go to people who know people. Career switchers probably won't know the right people in their new field, so they're going to have to create a new network. They may want to join professional organizations, get together in support groups with other job seekers, generally try to get in touch with what's called the "hidden job market."

GOLDBERG: Does the person who's had a career for many years have an advantage over a person just getting out of college if they're both looking for new careers?

GOLDSMITH: The older person is more mature and knows what it's like to be in the real working world.

GOLDBERG: I assume that most people have more contacts at thirty-five than they did at twenty-two.

GOLDSMITH: It depends on what kind of person you are and what kind of field you're in.

KABAT: Some people are in pretty isolated situations and have fewer contacts than someone who has the resources of a university. Also, someone in her thirties today probably had a very different experience when she first got her job eight or ten years ago. She probably just knew somebody who knew somebody and got it very easily, didn't really have to sell herself. It's changed in the last few years— it's much more competitive now.

GOLDBERG: Let's talk about the job interview.

GOLDSMITH: The main issue is one of convincing the employer that you're for real, that you're not just there on a lark. The employer is going to commit a lot of time and energy and financial resources to train you if he or she takes you on as a new employee, so your commitment to your new career is of utmost importance.

KABAT: You're going to have to demonstrate some kind of track record, some way to build connections, so they'll know it isn't just a case of, "Yesterday I was really frustrated with my job, so I sent out all these resumés."

GOLDSMITH: If you've been an amateur stockbroker for the past five or ten years, if that's always been an interest of yours, that's what you highlight. "Yes, I was a social worker, but in the last ten years, I've made $150,000 in my investments, and before that I was treasurer for X organization. So you can see, this is a thread that's been running through my life. Now I want to put it to professional use."

GOLDBERG: Would it make any sense to educate that employer if he or she seems to be unsophisticated about how common career switching is?

KABAT: You can do that in a very tactful, cautious way. If you can be very positive and self-confident about why you're changing, the employer will pick up on that.

GOLDBERG: Can you sell synergism? Can you say, "I think there may be some advantage to the fact that I was a social worker for all those years when it comes to investment counseling. I probably know people better than anybody on this floor because of my background."

GOLDSMITH: Definitely. That would be a convincing argument. But most of all you're selling yourself. That's a cliché, but it's all the more true in a career-switching situation. You don't have specific skills and training to offer, so above all else you're selling your potential.

GOLDBERG: How about this: "I want this job. I'm giving up a great deal to go into this field starting at the bottom. I wouldn't do that unless I really wanted it." That way the employer will know he or she is getting a very motivated person.

KABAT: That's an appropriate thing to say and an excellent argument, if it's really true. Each person has to find out what's true for him or herself and then say that in the interview.

GOLDBERG: Is career switching harder for a person who's in a specialized technical field than for a generalist?

GOLDSMITH: The generalist is more likely to be bringing the same skills to a new position.

GOLDBERG: Howard Figler, who wrote *The Complete Job-Search Handbook*, lists what he calls the ten hottest transferable skills. They are: budget management, supervising, public relations, coping with deadline pressures, negotiating and arbitrating, speaking, writing, organizing, interviewing, and teaching. Figler believes these skills can be offered to employers in totally different careers. Do you think that rings true?

KABAT: They are probably the ten easiest skills to transfer. You have to get *some* specific knowledge for any job, but if you begin with a combination of those ten, you could probably move to another career fairly easily and have some chance for moving up.

GOLDSMITH: Another skill I'd like to add to that list is problem-solving ability. But still, it always ends up being a matter of how well you sell yourself, how convincing you are, and how you *present* those skills.

GOLDBERG: I have a sense from the interviews I've done that people tend to switch back and forth between technical careers and people-oriented careers. Do you think I'm on to something?

KABAT: I think that's part of what's going on. Careers tend to be oriented toward data, people, things, or some combination of the three. At different points in people's lives, they have different interests. At some point, you might really want to work with people. Ten years later, you may have had enough of that and may be starved to work with data and ideas.

GOLDBERG: The other reason for switching careers that I hear mentioned a lot is to make more money. I hear that more now than I did some years ago.

KABAT: Again, part of that may be the baby boom. The bulk of our population is in the thirty-to-forty age range and that's a time when you want to own something. You want a house or you want a family, and that means you need more money. It's not okay anymore to make $5,000 a year in part-time jobs and go to school. You need stability.

GOLDBERG: Is it safe to say there's a conflict if you want more money and more contact with people? I picture the more lucrative careers as the ones with less involvement with people.

GOLDSMITH: It depends on what salary range you're talking about. If you're talking about a fast corporate track, then, yes, that's certainly eons from the earning potential of a social worker. Most people probably are comfortable somewhere between.

GOLDBERG: What are the issues that relate to families in a career switch?

GOLDSMITH: Money is a critical issue, because most people are going to face a pay cut if they're switching careers. They may end up taking a job that starts at an entry-level salary and bank on their potential earning power in the future.

GOLDBERG: That sounds like double trouble. Loss of esteem and loss of salary might make you a hard person to live with.

GOLDSMITH: One of the major reasons people don't switch careers is because they're locked into their present level of earnings.

GOLDBERG: Isn't that always an option?

GOLDSMITH: Not necessarily. If you have several children, you need a large home and your expenses are high. And a life-style choice that was made years ago, even if it no longer reflects your values or situation, may be extremely difficult to change.

GOLDBERG: What do you say to yourself, let alone your family, about a pay cut, about going back to the bottom of the ladder?

GOLDSMITH: Money's not everything.

KABAT: There has to be support from the family or it's probably not going to be successful. Statistically, that's even more true for women. If they don't have the support of the husband, they're not going to make it, because regardless of change, the woman is still the primary person responsible for the care of the home and the children. She'll need her whole family's support if she's going to work full-time or more. When you're changing careers, that's another issue: you're likely to be adding an extra time investment beyond the hours you're paid for.

GOLDBERG: Why?

KABAT: Chances are you can't complete a brand new job in the time they give you, so you'll take things home with you. If your family isn't sensitive, if they keep interrupting with, "Mom, where's the meal?" and that sort of thing, you're going to be sabotaged. You need their support, help, and understanding.

For the man, I think the issue is more whether the family can be emotionally supportive of his switch. The functioning of the household will probably change less.

GOLDBERG: What will his family get out of it? Let's say dad was an executive, bringing home $45,000 a year, and now he wants to be a therapist and he's going to start at $18,000 at a mental health center. What do they get out of it?

GOLDSMITH: They'll get a happier dad, someone who's possibly going to have more time to spend at home, want to spend more time at home, someone who's not as frazzled as business executives often are. Those are major trade-offs.

GOLDBERG: Can you generalize about whether men in their forties are switching to a faster or slower track?

GOLDSMITH: The ones who receive the most publicity are the ones who switch to a slower track. There's lots written about executives leaving their fast-track jobs and opening up hostels in Wisconsin or Connecticut or that sort of thing. Statistically, I'm not sure I can give you an answer to that question, but there's certainly movement both ways.

GOLDBERG: What about women?

KABAT: I would guess that the switch to a slower pace is more common in men. I don't see a lot of women who have been career women all their lives and then hit forty and say, "I want to go to a slower pace." Their issues are more, "How do I progress?" or "How do I stay where I am?"

GOLDBERG: For what type of personality is a career switch going to be hardest?

KABAT: I would say the very conventional, rule-oriented sort of person is going to have the hardest time with a career change. This type of person is going to be more impatient, more thrown by ambiguity.

GOLDBERG: What would you guess might be the number-one difficulty for women who are switching and the number-one difficulty for men?

GOLDSMITH: For men, it's probably the loss of income or ego or power. Those three things are really wrapped into one.

KABAT: For women, the crisis centers around family. Even a single women who doesn't have a family will think, "How much time is this career going to take? What if I decide to have kids when I'm thirty-six?" These questions can become a major barrier.

GOLDBERG: Should you expect that you might have to relocate?

KABAT: I don't know if you need to expect that you're going to have to relocate, but if you are not going to relocate, you might have to compromise. If someone were to say to me, "I want to make $20,000 and I want to stay in the Madison area and I'm going to teach," I'd have to say to them, "No, you're not. If you're going to stay in this area, you'll have to change either the amount you want to make or what you want to do."

GOLDBERG: How long should someone expect the process of the career switch to take?

KABAT: Depending on what area and whether the person has to stay in a job while he or she looks, it can be months or even years. If you have no experience in what you want to switch into, it may well take several years.

GOLDBERG: And is it helpful to read books about switching, or seek counseling or go to workshops?

KABAT: Again, it depends on the individual. One of the greatest things that people get from a group or reading a book is that they gain the self-confidence to go out and do it. A book is a starting point, and a support group can help you to get through the change, particularly if it takes a few years. But some people are very self-motivated and can do it on their own.

GOLDBERG: Any parting words about an attitude that might help people through the career switch?

GOLDSMITH: Be positive. Remember that if you're switching careers, you're selling yourself and your potential to an employer, and that's what you have to concentrate on. Be specific when you're relating what you've done to what you want to do. For the mathematician who wants to be a social worker, it's not enough to say to an employer, "I like people." You have to give them some examples of how that trait of liking people has manifested itself in your past jobs.

GOLDBERG: You've given us an overview of this subject that has opened my eyes in several ways. Let me repeat some of the major points we've discussed.

Most people will switch careers several times. It will be most helpful and can relieve a lot of stress and self-doubts to read something about career switching, join a support group, or talk with other people who have switched careers. If you don't talk to anybody, you're likely to wonder what's wrong with you. You will have to ask your family for their support and understanding, and family roles and circumstances might change considerably, particularly if you take a wage reduction in your new job. There are a few hints for the career switchers to pay attention to in writing a resumé and preparing for a job interview, but above all, it's confidence about and commitment to the career change that will be convincing to someone in a hiring position.

PART TWO

♦ ♦ ♦

Informational Interviews

CHAPTER 8

Advertising Account Executive

I would say that the advertising business can turn you into
a workaholic, and workaholics do excel in advertising. My
wife and my three daughters add a semblance of reality to
what can at times be a very unrealistic world of worry, of
living in a creative campaign that's going to be produced
next week, or a direct mail campaign that didn't work last
week.

—Matt Joyce

SUZY SCHOLFIELD-SANKS and MATT JOYCE are account executives working in advertising agencies. That field and that occupation have been given a somewhat glamorous reputation by the contemporary media. According to that image, the pace is fast, the competition fierce, and the stakes high. Matt and Suzy work, respectively, for a large and a small agency, and though their backgrounds would have logically led them in other directions, they have developed considerable expertise about their professions and can testify as to its real strains and rewards.

GOLDBERG: What does an account executive do?

SCHOLFIELD-SANKS: At our agency, an account executive works with clients and sells ideas.

GOLDBERG: Isn't it the copywriters who actually come up with the ideas and the account executives who act as liaisons between the copywriters and the clients? I would think that you are hired mostly as a salesperson and to do some hand holding with nervous clients, but not for your creative input. Is that right?

SCHOLFIELD-SANKS: Not for me, but it depends on the structure of the agency. We're a smaller agency and don't have an extensive creative staff, so the account executives are often responsible for coming up with ideas.

GOLDBERG: You work with about ten other people at Montzingo and Carmen Advertising. Matt, at Stephan and Brady, where you work, how many people are on the staff?

JOYCE: Around forty.

GOLDBERG: Would you describe the role of an account executive in your firm?

JOYCE: In the business area where I work, the account executives develop programs to sell a particular product or service to another company, which in turn uses that product or service to manufacture another product, which will be sold to a consumer.

GOLDBERG: Then you are partly responsible for the ideas, the concept of how you're going to sell, the creative part of advertising?

JOYCE: Yes, to a certain extent. We don't so much come up with the creative strategy as guide the process through the creative and production departments. And we're the middle persons between the agency, which generates and develops the ideas, and the client, who has final say and who eventually pays the bill.

GOLDBERG: It sounds to me like your job is a very difficult one, because you're a go-between. You have to present the client's needs to the creative department and the creative department's work to the client. Isn't a lot of your job really to keep that client happy?

JOYCE: To a great degree it is, but I would add a qualifier. Sometimes clients are happy with something that isn't very effective in moving their business. They may prefer one idea when another would generate more sales for them. And sometimes you give the creative department a direction for a particular campaign and they come back with ideas that are totally off the wall. With both the client and the creative department, there are a lot of subjective judgments and false starts, and it really comes down to your call in the long run about what will move the client's business forward.

GOLDBERG: If you compare a three-hundred-person agency in New York City to a five-person agency in Dubuque, will the account executive at the small agency have a lot more creative work to do? I would guess that at the big agency, the account executive is really walking a kind of tightrope between the creative departments and the client. Can we generalize that the bigger the agency, the less creative work an account executive will do?

JOYCE: I would agree with that.

GOLDBERG: Would you like to trade places with Suzy? Would you rather work for a small agency, where you get your fingers into more things?

JOYCE: I think not, because in my situation, on certain projects, I'm *the* creative person, *the* research person. I have an opportunity to really have some hands-on. . . .

GOLDBERG: As much as you want?

JOYCE: I think so. The balance in my situation is challenging and enjoyable.

GOLDBERG: Would you like to be an account executive in one of the huge agencies?

JOYCE: No, I wouldn't. The first thing I wouldn't like would be the hour-and-a-half commute every day. The larger agencies are almost always located in large cities and I wouldn't want to live in a large city. Second, I wouldn't want to have to deal with all the interdepartmental lines of communication that seem to be part of a very large agency. That would take up a great deal of my time.

As for the creative role of the account executive in a larger agency, I would have to play the role of devil's advocate with the people in the creative department, challenging them from the standpoint of the client. In a smaller agency, everyone is on a first-name basis and everyone works more as a team. And you don't have to worry about backgrounding the creative department all the time, because usually they'll have been working with the same clients for quite a while. Everyone's looking in a forward direction.

GOLDBERG: Why would someone want to work for a large agency?

SCHOLFIELD-SANKS: My first reaction is that they may feel there's more status involved.

GOLDBERG: How about money?

JOYCE: I'm not so sure that working for a large agency would get you more money. It may get you an opportunity to advance more quickly, though, just because of the greater number of employees who work there.

GOLDBERG: Matt, describe your typical day, if there is such a thing.

JOYCE: My typical day is about 50 percent organization and 50 percent punt. A great deal of my time is spent every day reviewing creative concepts, copy, the actual creative product. A certain part of that time is also spent figuring out the rationale, why we're doing a certain project in a particular way. Another thing I do is plan how our products and concepts will be presented to our clients. And I spend a great deal of time in some form of communication: reading, writing, or speaking.

The other half of my time is spent on client or account service. I talk with clients, get background for the projects we're working on, or go over information that the client has given me. If it's highly technical, I might rewrite it for the copywriters.

GOLDBERG: Suzy, is your time spent the same way, with half the day involved with concepts to sell the product and the other half working with your client?

SCHOLFIELD-SANKS: With me, it's probably a third working with clients, a third working internally with other people on the staff, and a third with suppliers.

GOLDBERG: Who are suppliers?

SCHOLFIELD-SANKS: Media reps. People who come to me and sell TV time, radio time, and space in print.

GOLDBERG: So you do some of the buying of the time?

SCHOLFIELD-SANKS: Yes. We have no media director on our staff.

GOLDBERG: What are the people around you like, the other account executives? Do you like them?

SCHOLFIELD-SANKS: Some I do, some I don't.

GOLDBERG: If you had to generalize about what kind of people account executives are, what would you say?

SCHOLFIELD-SANKS: I don't think they are any one particular kind of person. I will say, though, that all account executives that I've ever met have had a proven ability to communicate in the written and verbal form.

JOYCE: I'd say they're optimistic extroverts. They're outgoing and they enjoy talking and communicating. Optimism is very important, too, particularly when you do a project and it doesn't work quite as the client had expected. You always have to try and find the silver lining in those situations.

GOLDBERG: You're describing the personality of a good salesperson. Are account executives salespeople?

SCHOLFIELD-SANKS: I think they're salespeople in the truest sense of the word.

JOYCE: I agree.

GOLDBERG: What are they selling?

SCHOLFIELD-SANKS: They're selling the agency, always. I don't think the account executive ever stops selling the agency to the client. Because the nature of the business is very volatile, you can lose that account tomorrow.

GOLDBERG: Aren't you always scared, though? Here you are, getting paid a percentage of the advertising you generate, trying to please your clients all the time, and knowing that they could choose another agency any minute.

SCHOLFIELD-SANKS: I've developed what I feel is a very close relationship with my clients. Maybe I'm being optimistic, but I don't thing that they would do that.

GOLDBERG: Why wouldn't they do that? What do you do that's different than other account executives who sometimes lose accounts?

SCHOLFIELD-SANKS: My clients and I don't always agree, but I think I've built up a certain amount of trust and loyalty. I try to provide them with a lot of constructive ideas and persuade them that I'm right. Sometimes I'm not, but I like to think that most of the time I am.

I do feel like a psychologist in my job, and I think, as you mentioned before, there's sometimes some hand holding. Sure, accounts are going to leave, but a big part of my job is working to develop a good relationship, a foundation that will make that unlikely.

GOLDBERG: You both have college degrees. Your degree, Matt, is in—?

JOYCE: Agricultural journalism. And I have a rather extensive background in ecology and natural resources.

GOLDBERG: Ecology and natural resources! Is that at all helpful to you?

JOYCE: Yes, it is. In agricultural journalism, I was dealing primarily with hard facts: who, what, when, where, why—five journalistic W's. Now when I do a project for a client and I have to come up with an objective for the actual project, I apply the analytical skills I learned in journalism. I ask who, what, when, where, and why? And I come up with a strategy, a how.

In the natural resources area, my primary training was in ecology, and there was a time when I took a somewhat radical stand against companies that were polluting environments. Now I'm working with companies that make products directly related to environmental control, pollution-abatement programs, doing away with synthetic chemicals, and so on. My background in ecology allows me to translate highly technical scientific papers for potential customers or users of the product.

GOLDBERG: Suzy, your degree is in—?

SCHOLFIELD-SANKS: Radio, TV, and film.

GOLDBERG: Is that background helpful to you professionally?

SCHOLFIELD-SANKS: Not really, other than the awareness I developed about the broadcast business.

GOLDBERG: Do you wish you'd had a different background to prepare you for advertising?

SCHOLFIELD-SANKS: No. Even today I wouldn't major in advertising.

GOLDBERG: Why not?

SCHOLFIELD-SANKS: Because I think to be an effective person in the advertising business, it's important to know a little bit about a lot of different things.

GOLDBERG: So a liberal arts education is a good one for your profession?

SCHOLFIELD-SANKS: I think so.

GOLDBERG: Do you agree with that, Matt?

JOYCE: Yes, I do.

GOLDBERG: Besides having the qualities you already mentioned—the ability to sell ideas and the positive outlook—what kind of person do you think is right for the advertising business?

SCHOLFIELD-SANKS: Someone who's flexible and adaptable.

JOYCE: Someone who's organized.

SCHOLFIELD-SANKS: Someone who has a good sense of humor and can think quickly. And you have to be able to sell ideas internally and externally, to the staff and to the client. Believe me, those are two different types of salesmanship.

GOLDBERG: A diplomat?

SCHOLFIELD-SANKS: You've got to play politics a little bit.

JOYCE: Also someone who does not believe in a nine-to-five job. You hear it said that people in the advertising business are workaholics. It's not so much that they want to be, it's that they have to be. The business can be with you twenty-four hours a day. "Did I do this right? What did I forget to do? What am I going to do tomorrow?"

So you have to develop the ability to unplug from this business. It's very important to be able to stand back and get away, and to have some portion of one's self that is not tied up in the advertising business.

GOLDBERG: Is the pressure there all the time? When you go home? On weekends?

SCHOLFIELD-SANKS: I don't carry it with me. I've developed a sense of humor about it, and I think that comes from maturing and developing some security with the accounts that you work on. If I saw a spot blown this weekend for one of my clients, I would probably laugh about it and deal with it on Monday.

GOLDBERG: You're describing a career that you're never free of until the job's done. Which means if it's two in the morning, and an idea occurs to you that relates to your job, you're still "on duty." Do you wake up thinking about work in the middle of the night?

JOYCE: That can be the best time for creative ideas. And I've given up trying to go back to sleep. I get up and I write it down or work it out. It could be the one idea that you've been missing for a week in all the review sessions with your creative people. When it hits you, you have to write it down. I have a pad of paper and a flashlight next to my bed. It doesn't bother me to get up in the middle of the night and create.

GOLDBERG: You must be single.

JOYCE: No. I'm married and have three kids.

GOLDBERG: It doesn't bother your wife?

JOYCE: I think she's learned to adapt and live with it. It certainly bothers her.

GOLDBERG: Are you married, Suzy?

SCHOLFIELD-SANKS: Yes.

GOLDBERG: Does this job have any effect on your family life?

SCHOLFIELD-SANKS: It doesn't have any effect on my family life. I'm married to a professional who probably spends more time on his job than I spend on mine.

GOLDBERG: If you were a superworkaholic, wouldn't it?

SCHOLFIELD-SANKS: Probably, but I'm not.

GOLDBERG: How can you succeed if you're not? We're hearing

that you really have to be a workaholic to make it as an account exec.

SCHOLFIELD-SANKS: I don't agree with that. I devote a lot of time to other committee work and organizations outside of my day-to-day work and I spend time during weekdays doing volunteer work.

JOYCE: I would say that the advertising business can turn you into a workaholic, and workaholics do excel in advertising. My wife and my three daughters add a semblance of reality to what can at times be a very unrealistic world of worry, of living in a creative campaign that's going to be produced next week, or a direct mail campaign that didn't work last week.

GOLDBERG: I'm still not clear, Suzy, on how you succeed without having some of these workaholic tendencies that Matt describes. Can you ever be on top of your field without being that kind of person?

SCHOLFIELD-SANKS: I feel that I am on top of my world now. I'm doing what I want to do and I think I work with some of the best clients in this area. I'm challenged by them and I believe that I challenge them. If something comes up with a client over a weekend or at five o'clock, I'm the first to stay and handle that problem, but I don't need to take it all home with me.

GOLDBERG: Is your typical workday pretty much nine to five?

SCHOLFIELD-SANKS: For me it is—about a forty-hour week.

JOYCE: Mine isn't. Usually it's about forty to fifty hours, but there are some weeks when I work seventy or eighty hours. Also, there's another side to that coin. Certainly you have crunch projects, but there are other times when you take time. Our agency, for example, has Friday afternoons off all summer, and that's a good incentive to get most of your work done during the week.

GOLDBERG: What kind of salary can someone expect to make as an account executive?

JOYCE: The overall range is about $25–30,000 a year. It will vary depending on your years of experience and the area you're going to specialize in, whether it's fast foods or dry goods or what have you. But the top account executives make around $35,000 before they move up to an account-supervisor role, where they supervise account executives.

GOLDBERG: And how likely is that? How is the upward mobility?

JOYCE: It's very good.

GOLDBERG: In your firm of forty, is there someone who is an account supervisor?

JOYCE: We have a number of account supervisors.

GOLDBERG: So that would be your next step upward. And what does an account supervisor make?

JOYCE: Probably in the range of $30–40,000.

GOLDBERG: Where are those big six-figure salaries that we imagine people in advertising make?

JOYCE: In the biggest firms, in upper-management positions like vice-president or executive vice-president of account service, you start getting into the six-figure areas.

GOLDBERG: Suzy, where do you think you'll be in five years, if all goes well with your career?

SCHOLFIELD-SANKS: I hope that I'm doing what I'm doing now. I don't want to be an account supervisor.

GOLDBERG: Why not?

SCHOLFIELD-SANKS: Because the most important thing to me and the thing I get the most joy from is working very closely with my clients. I don't want to lose that. Having a client get excited about an idea and having that idea work—that's the ultimate. There's a lot of satisfaction in that.

GOLDBERG: What's the best part of the job for you, Matt?

JOYCE: The very best part of my job is having a client say to me, "Okay, what are we going to do next year?"

GOLDBERG: Being validated. I take it, then, the worst part of your job is when someone says, "I'm switching agencies."

JOYCE: That's a downer!

GOLDBERG: What's the worst part for you, Suzy?

SCHOLFIELD-SANKS: The worst part of it is knowing in your heart that the ideas that you have are right for the client, and having him disagree with you.

GOLDBERG: How do you get clients?

SCHOLFIELD-SANKS: We may hear that a client is unhappy with another agency, or we may hear through word of mouth of someone who needs advertising help. And we have an audiovisual presentation for prospective clients that describes our services.

GOLDBERG: It sounds like a dog-eat-dog kind of thing, going after another agency's business.

JOYCE: At times it is. And it's often easier to work with a company that has an existing ad agency, because there's a great deal of effort involved in educating a company that does not have any kind of an agency. You spend a lot of your time convincing them of the value of advertising.

GOLDBERG: And if they have an agency, you go after them anyway, which means that *your* accounts are being hustled all the time by other advertising agencies.

JOYCE: Precisely. Accounts come from a number of areas. You may go out and give an active pitch to a new company. You may have a creative idea that you think is very well suited to a particular company and you'll approach them even though they have another agency. Sometimes people will call you out of the blue. They'll go through the Yellow Pages, or they'll ask another firm if they know an advertising agency with a certain kind of expertise. So clients can come from anywhere, and clients can go anywhere.

GOLDBERG: What would you suggest to someone whose degree is not related to advertising, but who wants to move into the advertising business? What steps does this person need to take to become an account executive?

SCHOLFIELD-SANKS: I would suggest starting with a communications job in a company, a corporation, or a nonprofit organization. If you do this for a couple of years, you'll get the communications background you need. I also have a lot of colleagues who started at the bottom of an ad agency, as a receptionist or a secretary. In most ad agencies there are lots of people coming and going and it's fairly easy to move up if you show interest and skill.

GOLDBERG: How can you move up? How can you make your talents known?

SCHOLFIELD-SANKS: You may ask to do bits and pieces, you may say, "Gee, I'd like to help you on that project." It's very conceivable that you would have that opportunity.

GOLDBERG: So, if you have the attributes we discussed earlier, and you just get your foot in the door, sooner or later, with a little assertiveness, you can rise to a good position.

SCHOLFIELD-SANKS: I think so.

GOLDBERG: Let me try to summarize the major points you've made today.

The duties of account executives vary depending on the size of the agency they work for, but their essential role is to be the agency's representative to its clients. The amount of creative input they have varies from one agency to another. The typical personality of a successful account executive is upbeat and outgoing, and though a broad background is helpful, skill in communication is most essential. Salary and mobility are good, but you can expect to put in long hours.

CHAPTER 9

Public Relations Specialist

You've got to be able to write. That's number one. And you
must be able to get along well with all different types of
personalities. You need to be very diplomatic and cool under pressure and in a crisis, and you need to be pleasant.
You should be able to deal with people in a very upbeat and
positive way.

—*Lori Rappe*

> LORI RAPPE and TIM WARNER have jobs that are concerned
> with image and publicity, but they are also concerned with
> health care, tourism, and pizza. They work in public relations,
> a field that, ironically, has had its own image problems. Is it
> the job of the public relations specialist to glorify the mundane,
> to fool an unsuspecting public? Lori and Tim speak to this issue
> from different perspectives. Lori, who got her bachelor's de-
> gree in English with a minor in music, works for an advertising
> agency and represents a variety of clients. Tim has a bachelor's
> degree in journalism and is the director of public relations for a
> hospital in downtown Madison, Wisconsin.

GOLDBERG: Besides hospitals and ad agencies, what kind of organizations employ public relations personnel?

RAPPE: Every kind of organization from big corporations to
grass-roots coalitions. And there are specializations within public
relations: corporate, financial, media and press, special events. So a
PR person might work for a general agency, but he or she might also
work for an agency that specializes in any one of those areas.

GOLDBERG: Am I correct in assuming that almost any big organization has a public relations department?

WARNER: I think so. The size of the department will vary quite a bit depending on the institution, but most large organizations do have some sort of public relations department. And recently, many of them have changed the names of those departments, particularly hospitals and large corporations. They're calling them "community affairs" or "community relations" departments. That's probably because public relations has not had a real good public relations image itself.

GOLDBERG: Do you feel that public relations as a career has gotten a bum rap?

WARNER: Definitely. Many people think that PR people are there to cover up mistakes and make the bad guys seem like good guys. And really that's not true, though we certainly are in charge of putting the best foot forward for our clients. Our role is really very organized and planned. We don't just step in when there's a crisis.

RAPPE: It's more like a control of information, controlling the flow and the kind of information that's publicized about an organization. We're not trying to cover anything up, but we do try to create an image or an awareness of an organization. Sometimes we deal with an incorrect perception or a problem. The Tylenol scare is a good example of effective PR. The way those people handled public relations for that product after the tampering scare was phenomenal. Their sales are just as good today as they've ever been.

GOLDBERG: Simply put, what is the job of public relations?

RAPPE: From the agency point of view, it means dealing with a diverse number of clients, each of whom has a problem or an objective to accomplish. The public relations person identifies the client's objectives: the type of information to be disseminated, who gets the information, and what that's supposed to accomplish.

We sit down with every client and develop a strategy. Once that's done, the public relations person becomes a liaison between that client and its specific sector of the public, whether it's a particular consumer group or the public at large. We might deal with one particular medium—radio, newspaper, TV, or magazines—but generally, we deal with all of them.

GOLDBERG: What kinds of objectives do your clients have?

RAPPE: There are as many objectives as there are clients. An organization might have an image problem or an awareness problem.

Maybe nobody knows it exists. It might simply want publicity, just want its name in the paper. I work for the Wisconsin Dells, and they really don't have any problem to overcome. They just offer attractions and want people to come up and see them in the summer. So their objective is to promote tourism, and for me, that's just strict publicity.

GOLDBERG: They just want a lot of press for free?

RAPPE: Right. But on the other hand, I work for the Dean Medical Center, and they've recently developed HMO's, health maintenance organizations. People don't understand what those are, so I have to develop an educational strategy. I have to explain what an HMO is and how to choose one, and at the same time, promote the image of Dean as being helpful and caring and having a history within our community.

GOLDBERG: Does public relations ever take the form of paid advertising?

WARNER: No. It's never paid for. That's advertising, a different field altogether, though often they go hand in hand. In my role in my organization, I do advertising and public relations and marketing, everything rolled up into one. That's often the case, though in an agency type of setting, advertising people and public relations people will be separate.

RAPPE: The fact that PR isn't paid for is really the biggest difference, I think, because it can be rather commercial, like advertising is. Your client wants you to promote a product and you do that on his behalf, but whatever "ink," as it's called, you get for him is free. You get paid by the client, of course, but you never pay the newspaper or magazine or radio station to print your information or put it on the air. That's the difference between a public service announcement and a paid advertisement.

GOLDBERG: You work in an advertising agency, Lori. Can you describe how your job is similar or different from other people in that agency? What's a day like for you?

RAPPE: It's similar in that we all deal with different clients, many different clients. So my job is very diverse. I have a tourism client, I have a medical client, I have a pizza client. I have to understand all these different businesses, and my day is involved with juggling their needs and concerns and dealing with the appropriate media involved with each.

GOLDBERG: Do you spend most of your time on the phone?

RAPPE: There's a great deal of phone work. There's also a great deal of writing, and writing skill is one of the basics that you absolutely must have to be in the profession.

Most of my day is spent laying down foundations, laying down groundwork for my programs so that two months or six months down the road, I can start realizing some results. That means writing and phone work and it means becoming familiar with the editors and members of the media that I'm going to be dealing with. I do newsletters for my clients, I do various and sundry little details and projects on a daily basis, and I do administrative work as well. I also do conference reports and budgeting.

So a typical day involves a little bit of each one of those things. It's very interesting in that it's such a diverse profession.

GOLDBERG: Is your day very different, Tim?

WARNER: When I come into the hospital every morning, I really never know what's going to happen that day. I might have a whole schedule planned, with meetings every hour on the hour. Suddenly, at nine-thirty, I'll find out that something happened in our operating room and we're embroiled in some sort of controversy. And for the next three days, that may be all I'll work on. I'll do television interviews and radio interviews and talk to people from the press. So, you have to be able to react quickly, put everything else aside, and still come back to it when the excitement's over.

GOLDBERG: Are you the only public relations person at your hospital?

WARNER: No, we have three in public relations, which is probably an average-size staff for a large hospital. Smaller hospitals would probably have one person who would divide his or her time between public relations and personnel or volunteer services. But most large organizations do have at least two or three people.

GOLDBERG: Are you the boss of the three?

WARNER: Yes, I am.

GOLDBERG: So you have two employees?

WARNER: That's right, and I report directly to the administrator of the hospital. That's important because it means that what we do is considered upper-management function, and we have access to all the top goings-on of the organization. That's really critical to any sort of public relations function.

GOLDBERG: Lori, in public relations for an advertising agency, what is the best and the worst part of each day?

RAPPE: I think the best part of a day is when I'm starting to get results, when my phone calls are proving fruitful, I'm reaching people, getting interviews, accomplishing what I set out to accomplish for my clients. A bad day is when it appears that I won't accomplish what I set out to do, or when a crisis occurs that I don't think I handle very well, or when I have problems with a member of the staff.

GOLDBERG: What kind of problems come up with the staff at your advertising agency?

RAPPE: My supervisor and I are the only two people at the agency in public relations, and although there are a lot of similarities between advertising and public relations, there are also certain differences. Not all advertising executives have a good understanding of what public relations is and what it can do. So sometimes, just because of a lack of understanding, they don't see that what you've done is the best way to do it, is the correct public relations approach. I fight that all the time.

GOLDBERG: So it's a Rodney Dangerfield problem: you don't get no respect.

RAPPE: I don't get no respect, no. It's frustrating.

GOLDBERG: How about in your situation, Tim?

WARNER: When I'm really in control of the situation, when I'm involved in planning a product, setting objectives, carrying through and seeing results—that's when I really feel good. It's when I get involved in just one part of the total process that things seem to go wrong.

GOLDBERG: Describe the kind of person who is likely to be successful and happy working in public relations.

RAPPE: You've got to be able to write. That's number one. And you must be able to get along very well with all different types of personalities. You need to be very diplomatic and cool under pressure and in a crisis, and you need to be pleasant. You should be able to deal with people in a very upbeat and positive way.

GOLDBERG: You mentioned before this interview that you're a little high-strung. I wonder, since you said you have to have such a cool head in a crisis, whether that's a problem.

RAPPE: I maintain my composure and my professionalism, because I am a professional. I deal with each crisis calmly and then I go to my office and shut the door and kick the wall for about half an hour. That's how I deal with it.

GOLDBERG: Do you kick the wall, too, Tim? Do you find that you have to keep the lid on a lot when you really don't want to?

WARNER: Definitely. Being a public relations professional requires that. Sometimes you're interrogated by a reporter and what you want to say is, "Get out of my life! I don't want to talk to you anymore!" But you have to answer questions and provide information and be pleasant.

GOLDBERG: Do you sometimes have to deal with antagonistic reporters?

WARNER: On occasion, and it's really important never to burn a bridge.

GOLDBERG: When you're feeling the pressure that you're both describing, does it affect your family life, your personal life?

RAPPE: I don't have a family, so what I find it does to me is make me feel very lonely. There aren't too many people in this profession, and people who aren't can't really understand it. So I can't run in and throw PR jargon all around the room and talk about my problems. And the misconceptions about PR and PR people are rampant. I went apartment hunting recently and got turned down because, since I'm in public relations, landlords think I must have a lot of parties.

GOLDBERG: I take it the institutional PR jobs—working for a corporation or a hospital as you do, Tim—lend themselves more to a stable nine-to-five life than ad agency PR work.

WARNER: Not necessarily. My first job out of college was in an agency, so I've worked in both environments, and both really go beyond nine-to-five. Certainly at the hospital, we can suddenly get very busy and work a lot of extended hours, but it tends to even out. Sometimes I don't go in until eight-thirty in the morning.

GOLDBERG: Not until eight-thirty! What time do you usually start?

WARNER: In the hospital people usually start at six-thirty. It can be really demanding, but I think it's a profession that can be managed. You can have a family and be a very hardworking public relations professional.

GOLDBERG: How available are careers in public relations?

RAPPE: The careers are there, the problem is identifying them. People trying to enter the field have an unrealistic expectation about the level at which they can enter. They want to be an account executive or a junior account executive or an assistant. Those jobs are the ones you get promoted to after you get your feet wet.

I think people entering this field should look for a position that's lower than what they ideally want. It's so important to get that precious foot in the door. Unless you're willing to take less than your ideal job, you're not going to get your opportunity. I've heard stories about people starting in the mail room and eventually owning their own companies. It does happen and it seems to happen a lot in our profession.

GOLDBERG: Let's say you have a bachelor's degree in English. You're bright, you're a good writer, a good communicator. What kind of PR job might you find?

WARNER: There are a lot of entry-level jobs in public relations. That's one of the good things about the profession, and one reason for it is nonprofit and other small organizations that can't afford to pay very well. Those jobs become available to new graduates and they're an excellent place to start. That kind of organization frequently has all types of different responsibilities, which means you can learn the trade working for them. You'll work long hours, you won't be paid much, and sometimes you'll feel that your job is not all that important, but it's great experience.

GOLDBERG: Is it possible to create your own job by going to smaller companies that don't have a PR department and saying, "I've got an idea for you . . ."

RAPPE: That would be difficult to do without experience, without a background.

WARNER: It's very important that a person go out while still in college and really hustle for experience. There are lots of ways to get good writing experience, good organizational and special-events experience. Having that background will also give a potential employer a lot better feel for what you can and cannot do.

RAPPE: We should mention the Public Relations Student Society of America. It's a major group with branches in lots of cities around the country; any student can join. Another good organization is Women in Communications, which assists women who are making career changes or who are newly graduated and looking for careers in communications.

GOLDBERG: Do you have other tips for finding entry-level positions in public relations?

WARNER: It's important to do a thorough assessment of the job market in your area, and it's best, if possible, to have a very broad outlook as to *where* you might work.

A good place to start is with major organizations and corporations, because they have larger public relations staffs and can often afford to hire and train a young person.

GOLDBERG: Would you suggest going to a corporation cold, or only if you're responding to an ad?

WARNER: I think the best way to find a job is to do some homework on a corporation or an agency or a company, find out what they're about, talk to a few people who work there, and really get a feeling for what their needs might be. Then write or call the person who is the most appropriate for you to talk to.

RAPPE: I'm always impressed by the candidates who call up and want an appointment to show me something they've done as opposed to just sending a resumé. They come in and they show me school assignments and projects they've worked on and I get a sense of their abilities and who they are. Being assertive is good PR. Those are the people I consider first.

Also people trying to get into public relations had better be extra careful about the way they do their resumés and their initial approach, because they are approaching the people who approach people.

WARNER: And it's very important to be into the network of public relations. Sooner or later, an opening will come up and because you've been talking to people and people have seen your projects, you're much more likely to be considered than the person who just sends a resumé across the desk.

RAPPE: I would suggest, too, that people looking for PR jobs start in larger markets, larger cities, where they'll find more of the types of businesses that we're talking about.

GOLDBERG: Lori, you've been in PR five years. Are you making a good living?

RAPPE: Yes. Between $20–30,000.

GOLDBERG: Tim, you've been working in PR for how long?

WARNER: About seven years. And I'm in the same range, $20–30,000. That's a decent living, considering my degree and my experience. Public relations has a lot of potential. Our highest earning years are definitely yet to come. We don't top out early, like some professions do.

GOLDBERG: What can a hot-shot PR person make?

WARNER: I was reading a newspaper story the other day about one of the major corporations in the state. Their public relations person was the vice-president of corporate affairs and was making about $225,000. Now that's a very hot-shot public relations professional, but there are certainly people out there in corporations who are making $50,000; it's not all that uncommon.

GOLDBERG: What might an entry-level PR person start at?

RAPPE: Realistically, one can expect to start at around $13–15,000.

GOLDBERG: Tim, you're currently director of public relations for a hospital. What's ahead for you?

WARNER: The health care industry is becoming much more involved in marketing and public relations, so there's really a lot of growth potential.

GOLDBERG: And for you, Lori?

RAPPE: There's growth potential to various supervisory capacities as well as to independent consulting, which is sort of the cream at the top.

GOLDBERG: Any last suggestions for a person who's in college and thinking of a public relations career?

RAPPE: Take courses in business, business administration, and marketing. More and more schools, thank heavens, are offering public relations courses of study. Join the student associations and do a lot of writing. If you can, get some articles placed in your local newspaper, and I would recommend taking not just journalism and English grammar–type courses, but also broadcast reporting, which is more typical of how PR people write.

WARNER: I would recommend that people have some experience in doing survey research and those types of things, because PR is moving more and more toward being a data-oriented profession. We're concerned with the evaluation of our projects, and with being able to do research up front to find out what our public thinks. That's the current direction.

GOLDBERG: To summarize: public relations is a field with good entry-level opportunities and good opportunities for advancement. Communication skills are essential and a background in journalism, media, and business are very helpful. Public relations can be stressful and regular business hours fall by the wayside when there's an emergency. The diversity of the job and the relatively good pay and upward mobility are compensating factors.

CHAPTER 10

Advertising Copywriter

It *is* a very high-pressure field. You can get ulcers from it,
but hey, it's a job. It seems your attitude is what will carry
you through. If you're basically a nervous or neurotic person, or if you get upset by small things, don't go into advertising. It would probably drive you right up the wall.
        —*Charlie Propson*

CHARLIE PROPSON and JIM ARMSTRONG both began their professional careers as teachers. Charlie earned her teaching certifi-
cate and a bachelor's degree in art from the University of
Wisconsin in Madison and began a teaching career in Australia. Jim taught while completing a book of poetry that became
his master's thesis. Now both are employed by the profession
that has brought us "the uncola," "ring around the collar," and
"Where's the beef?" The people who write these memorable
slogans and the texts that accompany them, who name products and services, and who promote brand X over brand Y are
advertising copywriters. They influence our lives, our individual and collective self-image, and especially our spending habits to an extraordinary degree. It's a career with distinct
elements of insecurity and competition, along with the possibility of succeeding or failing on a grand scale. The trade-off
seems to be the diversity and stimulation of working in a creative capacity with other creative people.

GOLDBERG: Help us become familiar with an ad agency. What

are the different professional careers that people might have there and what are the different labels for these careers?

PROPSON: Most of the marketing is worked out by the account executives. They work with the clients, discovering what their needs are and what will sell their products or get their message across best. Then they take what they've learned to the creative department, where the copywriters and the art directors work.

GOLDBERG: What do the copywriters do?

PROPSON: Copywriters are responsible for taking this information, distilling it, coming up with a message, and developing a strategy for getting that message across to the consumer or whoever the audience is. But we don't do that alone. We work in conjunction with an art director, so we're not the sole source of ideas. The art director designs the visual part of the ads, and we both work with the people in the media department, who select the publications or broadcast media in which the ads will appear.

GOLDBERG: Would you describe your typical day?

ARMSTRONG: There is no such thing as a typical day in advertising. It's impossible to plan a weekly schedule and almost useless to plan a daily schedule.

You might come in one morning planning to work on a certain project—let's say you're outlining a script for an industrial audiovisual program, and thinking of pictures that match the words. You'll have your cup of coffee and be all cozied up in your chair and gazing out the window contemplating industrial things, when all of a sudden a frantic account executive will storm into your office and say, "Oh, my God, we've got an ad that we've got to get out in two hours! The client's chomping at the bit, and if we don't meet the deadline the whole campaign's sunk!"

I'll ask him what it's got to do with and he'll say, "Well, we're selling carrots at fifteen cents a pound and the message has got to get out loud and clear." So you shift gears completely.

GOLDBERG: It sounds a little wild and a little chaotic. Charlie, is that your experience?

PROPSON: Exactly. I remember a time when I finished a recording session at seven o'clock at night and came back to the agency just to drop stuff off. A client was there, meeting with an account executive, and he insisted that he have a letter written for his sales staff by eight o'clock the next morning.

So I went home and stocked up on jujubes and popcorn and

worked until about two or three in the morning and walked in with it at eight. And that's not that unusual. Of course it doesn't happen all the time or we'd all have nervous breakdowns.

GOLDBERG: But it is a high-pressure business?

PROPSON: Very much so.

GOLDBERG: Your backgrounds don't directly relate to being in advertising. Jim, how did you begin?

ARMSTRONG: I was teaching at the university and was writing a book of poems that served as my master's thesis. I had made a decision not to go on for a Ph.D., but rather to get a job in the "real" world.

One day I was looking in the classified section of the paper and I saw an ad titled "Wordsmith." It was obviously written by a copywriter, because it made the job sound luscious: ". . . an idea person who loves words and can get people excited about words and can translate those words into vital selling images." I read that and I thought, "Gee, this is kind of close to writing a poem, *and* I can get paid for it."

The word *copywriter* was never mentioned until I met with the employer and then I kept thinking, "Copywriter . . . what in the world is a copywriter?" He explained what a copywriter does and gave me a couple of projects to take home, some ads to rewrite in five different ways.

So I rewrote the ads and he liked what he saw and I got the job. I didn't have to go through a lot of interviewing or talk to a lot of people. But I went in not knowing what I was applying for.

GOLDBERG: How many years ago was that?

ARMSTRONG: Five.

GOLDBERG: What did the job pay?

ARMSTRONG: When I started, $12,000.

GOLDBERG: Charlie, your story?

PROPSON: My starting salary wasn't that high. I graduated with a degree in art and got an education certification because my mother made me. She said, "Dear, you can *always* get a job teaching." And I did teach in Australia for two years, but it wasn't for me.

When I came back, I made a decision about work. I decided that although I wasn't born rich, I was born smart and I was going to get a job that I liked. It's very important to me to spend time doing what I want to do.

I thought that the art background was the way to go, so I came back to Madison, Wisconsin, and worked for Rennebohm's drug-stores, doing their newspaper layouts. I started at $1.75 an hour and I was really thrilled to get the job. I was their third choice; nobody else would take the job before me because the pay was too low, but I thought it was going to at least be some decent experience.

GOLDBERG: How did you move from layout to copywriting?

PROPSON: I had a terrific boss at the time, but he had been writing drugstore ads for twenty-five years and was very sick of it. When I asked him if I could do some of the writing myself, he was happy to help me out. He brought in his old textbooks, and I started digging up information on advertising at the library.

At the same time I had a friend in Chicago who was getting into copywriting. After a year and a half of work with Rennebohm's, I went to Chicago and showed her my portfolio, which included both writing and art samples. She gave me a few pointers on job hunting.

I did up a stack of resumés, one version for art jobs and one for writing jobs, and I was just about ready to send them out when four ads appeared in the paper. Two were for writing jobs, two were for art jobs. I sent out my resumé and got one response, from a local advertising agency. I interviewed with them and was hired. That was the start of my career.

GOLDBERG: So it wasn't a lot of magic when you really get down to it. You began with a low-paying job where you laid out newspaper ads, answered an ad for a copywriter, and got the job.

PROPSON: Right. And I had a lot of help from my friend with interviewing techniques and learning what advertising agencies look for. And I did do research into the field, so that I could talk about it intelligently.

GOLDBERG: What tips would you pass on to someone hoping to be hired to write ad copy?

ARMSTRONG: I hire copywriters now and often I'll ask them to go off on their own and put together mock ads. That does two things: it shows me if they're creative, and it shows me if they're genuinely interested. Eighty-five percent never come back again, but of the ones who do come back, about half show a lot of potential. And I think it's the interest and enthusiasm and drive that they have before they get the job that plant the seeds for success if they do get hired.

GOLDBERG: But you're suggesting they shouldn't come in and say, "I want to be in advertising," but rather, "I want to be a copy-writer" or "I want to be a media buyer." Is it best to be specific?

PROPSON: Yes, very much so. Everybody has potential in several areas, but when you're talking to a prospective employer, make sure that you're projecting just one image.

GOLDBERG: Is copywriting something that people can get into without any specific training in advertising? Someone with perhaps just a flair for writing?

PROPSON: I think it's entirely possible. The best thing to do is put together a book, a portfolio of your samples.

GOLDBERG: But if you've never done anything . . .

PROPSON: But you can do something; you don't have to wait for a prospective employer to ask you to write. You can even pick up a pen and write something in longhand, although it would be better to type it. It can be as few as eight to ten samples. Take an ad and do it differently or come up with an imaginary product and do the text for a print ad or a radio or television script. Don't worry about fancy artwork; an employer looking at your book will be able to imagine what it will look like with artwork.

GOLDBERG: And it's important to read about the field a little so you can talk about it when you interview?

PROPSON: Also just to know what you're getting into.

GOLDBERG: You both have degrees that are unrelated to advertising. What did you get from your liberal arts background that is valuable in your career today?

PROPSON: Just about everything is of value. I couldn't be a copywriter if I didn't have all that background in English and history and art.

ARMSTRONG: Exactly. As I mentioned earlier, you can be doing one thing in advertising and ten minutes later you might be doing something totally different. That's where the liberal arts background comes in, and the more varied your background the better.

GOLDBERG: Is the advertising world as stressful as the image we have of it from movies and television?

PROPSON: It *is* a very high-pressure field. You can get ulcers from it, but hey, it's a job. It seems your attitude is what will carry you through. If you're basically a nervous or neurotic person, or if you get upset by small things, don't go into advertising. It would probably drive you right up the wall.

GOLDBERG: What makes it so stressful?

PROPSON: Deadlines. People asking you to be in two places at the same time. People taking your beautifully written words and saying, "This doesn't fit the marketing strategy; we're going to have to do it over." Other people not coming through for you. Having $20,000 worth of camera equipment ready to shoot a TV commercial, and having the client say, "We can't get the product to you till Thursday." There are a lot of things that can add to the pressure.

GOLDBERG: Do you see a lot of high-strung people around you in the business?

ARMSTRONG: Yes, I do.

PROPSON: I think it can make you that way.

GOLDBERG: What qualities do you need to be a successful copywriter?

ARMSTRONG: You have to love words, love to play with them, and know how to make them effective. Grammar is usually irrelevant in advertising, but you have to be able to translate words into visual imagery and you have to want to have fun.

PROPSON: You have to have a bit of a business sense too. We have a writer in our office who gets so emotionally attached to his words that he forgets sometimes what the purpose of those words is, which is to get the message across, to sell products, to convince people to do or not to do something. That's very important.

GOLDBERG: Give us an example of an assignment you've had and how you resolved it.

ARMSTRONG: About a year and a half ago, we had a new client. He had no name for his company and his product was still in the production stages. He wanted us to name the product and develop a campaign of five different print ads, in full color, which would establish the product's name and an image at the same time. Plus, we had to come up with stationery, business cards, and a public relations program, and this had to be ready in six weeks.

GOLDBERG: What was your part?

ARMSTRONG: To name the company and come up with the concept for the newspaper ads.

GOLDBERG: How's the company doing?

ARMSTRONG: Going gangbusters.

GOLDBERG: You've got to tell us what the product is!

ARMSTRONG: The product is a disposable plastic tray, the kind you get on airlines.

GOLDBERG: And how did you come up with the name?

ARMSTRONG: When you look for names, you develop this sort of quadrant thing. You list benefits of the product up here, and features down there and the mood of the product over here and the target audience over there, in words that describe these aspects. And you try words together in different combinations. What we finally came up with was "BonFaire America." "America" because it's an American-based corporation whose major competition is overseas, and "BonFaire" because they wanted to have a European, continental flavor to their product.

GOLDBERG: Was it fun doing that, or was it pressured?

ARMSTRONG: It was fun. Very rarely do you get to name a company, let alone a product. And it's rare when you're not stuck with excess baggage that's been created for the client by another agency. When you can come in totally fresh, it's exciting.

GOLDBERG: Here you are now, in advertising, in the business world, getting excited by what you do. Would you ever have thought when you were in graduate school and writing poetry that you would do this, or would you have thought it was a sell-out?

ARMSTRONG: I struggle with that every day.

GOLDBERG: Why?

ARMSTRONG: When I go home and turn on the news at night and see bombings in Lebanon and hungry people in Pakistan, and I've been flying high all day because I did something like name a disposable plastic tray, then I wrestle with what I'm doing.

GOLDBERG: Do you wrestle with it, Charlie?

PROPSON: Not at all.

ARMSTRONG: Good for you. You're in much better psychological shape than I am.

GOLDBERG: If someone had told you when you were in college that you were going to be paid for coming up with ideas to sell products, would you have been comfortable with that?

PROPSON: No, because I'm a child of the sixties. At that point it would have just been the worst thing I could possibly do. But I don't look at it as a sell-out in the world that we're living in now, in my space and time. I'm a part of the business community; I'm serving a function for that business community.

Also, I can honestly say that I've never worked for any client that I felt badly about. I've had a couple of jobs that in hindsight maybe I wish I hadn't worked on, but at the time, I did them in good conscience. I've also had one opportunity in my career to refuse to work on something because it went against my personal beliefs, and I had no problems within my agency getting clearance for that.

So I've never done anything that I've felt really bad about and I have done a lot of things that I feel very good about, getting messages across, getting new products on the market. If you're going to be part of the business world, advertising is no worse place to be than any other. It's part of the mix.

GOLDBERG: Can you give me a range of what people who have been copywriters for four or five or six years might expect to make in a medium-sized market?

PROPSON: About $20–30,000.

ARMSTRONG: That's in a medium-sized market. In a big city, the sky seems to be the limit.

GOLDBERG: And what is the sky? Are we talking $100,000 a year?

PROPSON: Yes. My friend in Chicago is now making $70,000. And if you figure in bonuses, profit sharing, and all these things that go along with jobs in this profession, those extras can add up to a much larger salary.

GOLDBERG: Let's review some tips for people who want to find a job writing ad copy, but who have no training or background in that field.

PROPSON: Get together a book of samples; make them up yourself if necessary. And learn something about the business just by going to the library and reading about advertising.

GOLDBERG: Anything to add to that, Jim?

ARMSTRONG: I'd do it exactly the same way. Putting a book together also shows initiative, and that's the first thing that any employer is looking for.

GOLDBERG: Who should *not* go into this business, even if they have the knack of coming up with ideas to sell products? Even if they like words? Even if they're creative?

PROPSON: People who can't handle deadlines. It's critical to get projects done on time. There's no such thing in advertising as "I need an extension."

GOLDBERG: What's the future for copywriters? Do you see this as a growing field?

ARMSTRONG: Yes. We live in an information-based society.

PROPSON: Absolutely. Communication is "it" right now, with the move away from heavy industry and toward more high-tech fields. There's going to be an increasing need for people who can communicate what this new stuff on the market is all about.

GOLDBERG: Let me add a couple of things to your summary. A

liberal arts education seems to be an ideal background for an ad copywriter, because of its broad scope. Although you've emphasized that copywriting and the advertising world in general are stressful, you also used the word *fun* several times in describing what you do. Starting pay for copywriters is likely to be low, but successful and experienced copywriters can do very well financially. This is a profession for people who love words, who love excitement, and who can tolerate a considerable amount of pressure.

CHAPTER 11

Editor

I'll come up with an idea for a story and give it to a staff writer. He or she will do great research, but come back with a story that's not very well written or focused. I'll take this good research, this good legwork, give it focus and impact, and put it together into something that I know my readers are going to get excited about. That process is far more enjoyable and creative than I ever thought it would be.

—*Carol Wilson*

DOUG BRADLEY and CAROL WILSON work with words and create word products. They are editors. Doug works at Stanton and Lee, a publishing company with a special commitment to books written by Wisconsin residents or about Wisconsin subject matter. Carol edits two newsletters for Magna Publishing—"The National On-Campus Report" and "Athletic Director and Coach." What Carol and Doug have to say about editing will be reassuring to anyone who thinks of it as a rarefied occupation with few opportunities for entry.

GOLDBERG: When I think of jobs in editing, the first thing that comes to mind is a New York publishing house and about thirty editors working there, grinding away. . .

BRADLEY: In those little cubicles, with the green visors.

GOLDBERG: Yes. Is that in any way accurate?

BRADLEY: Not really. Editors today are involved in a wide variety of functions. We're moving away from that image.

GOLDBERG: I have a general idea of what an editor does. Would you give me some specifics?

BRADLEY: Carol and I might be able to draw some contrasts here because of the different genres that we're involved in. I work strictly with books, both fiction and nonfiction. And because I work for a small regional company, I do just about everything from line editing. . . .

GOLDBERG: What does that mean?

BRADLEY: Remember the old structure diagrams you did in school, where you identified the subject, predicate, and object of a sentence? I do that kind of thing. I make sure the sentence flows and the syntax is proper. On very technical kinds of things—we publish a gardening guide, for instance—I make sure that information is in step-by-step order and easy to follow. I work with authors, acquiring manuscripts, brainstorming with them about how their work should proceed, where it's strong, where it's weak, and how to make it better. And I help with decisions about the physical product and the production. A lot of books are sold on their appearance alone, so the graphic package must be appealing, must pop off the shelf.

GOLDBERG: Carol, in your work, do you wear a green visor?

WILSON: Never. I was given one as a young editor, but I've never been able to use it. Nowadays, you're more likely to get eyestrain from sitting at your video display terminal all day, moving around chunks of copy.

GOLDBERG: How does your work differ from Doug's?

WILSON: I edit newsletters oriented to various aspects of college life. My job includes determining the content of the newsletters, screening sources, interviewing, and lots of reading. We have to take a wide range of information and reduce it to a small package that our readers can go through quickly and easily.

GOLDBERG: Where do you start?

WILSON: We subscribe to daily newspapers and student newspapers from across the country, and to many newsletters and other forms of information from national organizations. We read these, decide what's pertinent to our specific audience, and boil that down to real nuggets. That's what we're selling our readers.

GOLDBERG: And what's your goal? Who are you trying to reach and what do you want to give them?

WILSON: "National On-Campus Report," for example, is about student activities. We want to be able to tell our readers what's happening on campus and off campus, so that they're up on trends, on problems that have hit campuses and that may be coming to their campus, or on good ideas that other people have had that they can put to use on their campus. It really covers the whole realm of nonacademic student activities, and our primary targets are the dean of students, the director of student affairs, those types of people. But we also go to student newspapers, student governments, counseling centers, just about anybody on campus.

GOLDBERG: And your income is through subscription?

WILSON: That's right. That's how most independently operated newsletters are run. Other newsletters are affiliated with specific organizations and there are a lot of editing jobs available there. Almost any national or even regional organization is going to put out a newsletter, and for that they're going to hire an editor. Those are excellent job opportunities.

Newsletters are also a good way for people to explore how to use editing skills in a field in which they're interested. If they look around long enough, they'll probably find a publication about their particular interest or hobby or field of expertise and they can try to become involved in that publication.

GOLDBERG: Would you describe your typical day for us, Carol?

WILSON: The first part of my day is usually spent dealing with mail and newspapers, doing a lot of reading. That generally takes about three and a half or four hours. The remainder of the day I contact people who have information for our stories, and help our staff plan those stories and put them together. I edit things written by other writers on my staff, and I do some writing on my own.

GOLDBERG: Is most of your time spent working with words or with people?

WILSON: Most of my time in this particular job is actually spent reading. Next would be working with people. We do a lot of interviewing over the phone and a lot of talking back and forth with other staff members, discussing stories. After that, I guess most of my time is spent dealing with the actual display terminal.

GOLDBERG: Are the computers intimidating?

WILSON: The computers we use are literally built to be used by idiots. They tell you every step of the way what to do next. It takes a while to learn the system and be comfortable with it, but actually the computer makes editing and writing so much easier and so much more fun than the old way—the typewriter or pencil—that you quickly get over your fears.

GOLDBERG: Do you use computers, Doug?

BRADLEY: Yes, but we haven't come into the computer age as quickly or completely as Carol has. I still bang out a lot of rewrites and correspondence on an old manual typewriter. We do use a word processor to correct manuscripts and occasionally, when we've had an author who's a distance away, we get our two machines talking rather than spending a lot of time on the phone or exchanging reams of correspondence.

GOLDBERG: Doug, maybe if you describe your typical workday, I'll understand whether this is basically a technological kind of job or a creative kind of job.

BRADLEY: I spend a substantial part of my day working with manuscripts and talking with authors. I might make general suggestions, for instance about how a portion of a book should flow, or I might be very specific. Sometimes I'll go line by line, crossing out and adding the red ink, cleaning it up, making the expression as solid and as informative as it can be. And depending on the stage that a manuscript's in, I might spend a substantial part of my day proofing galleys, which are the printed drafts of the manuscript.

We also have to be aware of where our markets are, what our readers are reading, what the public in general is reading. So I spend time looking at industry publications—*Publisher's Weekly* and magazines of that sort—to see what's popular, what the trends are.

I also meet with people about all kinds of things. Any day of the week, I might meet with a binder, a paper salesman, a marketer, a direct mail person, a printer, or somebody who's got a manuscript idea. Every day at some point, I'll have a meeting scheduled with another staff person or with somebody outside the office.

GOLDBERG: Is editing a nine-to-five job?

WILSON: The great thing about being an editor, I think, is that it can be a nine-to-five job if that's what you want, but it doesn't have to be. There's a great deal of flexibility depending on what kind of publishing house you work for, whether it's a newsletter publisher or a book or magazine publisher. Many newsletter editors work out of their homes, setting their own hours. It's a good field for the kind of flexible time schedules that are increasingly popular today.

GOLDBERG: Doug, would you say this is a good field for a workaholic?

BRADLEY: It can be, but it doesn't have to be. I like the point Carol made about flexibility. If you like a nine-to-five routine and that's where you function best, that's great, but it's not your only option.

When I initially got my job, the fellow who hired me and I were most attracted to each other because of our involvement in the rearing of our children. We had both quit our previous jobs to spend time at home with our kids while our wives went back to work and furthered their careers. Editing allowed me the flexibility to do a substantial amount of my work at home.

GOLDBERG: Are you allowed to be as creative as you'd like to be? Do you ever feel a frustration because you're always hewing other people's original ideas?

BRADLEY: No, I really don't feel that way. I pride myself on being a writer and I've done a substantial amount of free-lance writing, so I do work with my own original ideas. And my job does involve a lot of creativity: the engagement with other people, the flexibility I have with the material, and the understanding that we come to collectively in terms of where it should go and how it should get there.

GOLDBERG: The stereotype that I have of editors working alone in a cubbyhole all day. . . .

BRADLEY: It happens. It happens in my job. At some point, somebody—and if it's not the author, it's going to be the editor—has to sit down and go line by line and make sure that the manuscript is saying what it should.

GOLDBERG: I think a lot of people might hesitate to go into this field for fear that the editing process is very tedious.

WILSON: When I was in my early twenties, I was a reporter and I remember saying that I'd never be an editor. I did think it would be tedious and I enjoyed what I was doing, coming up with ideas and taking an idea and really researching it. Ten years later, I'm doing very little writing and I find that there's a whole different creative process involved in editing.

Now, I'll come up with an idea for a story and give it to a staff writer. He or she will do great research, but often come back with a story that's not very well written or focused. I'll take this good research, this good legwork, give it focus and impact, and put it together into something that I know my readers are going to get excited about. That process is far more enjoyable and creative than I ever thought it would be.

GOLDBERG: What are the most important skills you bring to being an editor?

WILSON: In my case I'd say good judgment is the first and foremost thing. "Campus Report" is eight pages long and it's published every two weeks. We probably throw away six pages of copy for every eight pages that we print, so I have to make a lot of decisions. The second most important thing is probably coming up with ideas that will interest our readers, being able to see a potential story for the newsletters in a newspaper clipping. And, of course, the ability to work with people and to communicate both verbally and on paper.

GOLDBERG: Should working with words be the first thing?

WILSON: Actually, I don't think so. You can often learn to work with words more easily than you can develop either a field of expertise in which you have the judgment you need or the ability to work with people. I think with a lot of work, you can learn the precision of language that's necessary to be a good editor.

GOLDBERG: Do you buy that, Doug?

BRADLEY: She's very convincing. I guess on my scale, the communication aspect is a little more important. I think you have to have a strength of communication. . . .

GOLDBERG: Written or verbal?

BRADLEY: Written and verbal. But I'd like to stress that to be an editor, I don't think it's as important that you have editing experience so much as experience related to writing and the writing process and the awareness of language that results from that.

The other quality that I think is important for an editor is the versatility that comes from having a broad background. You need that, first of all, to perform the variety of functions we've already mentioned, but just as important, a rich background enhances your judgment. As Carol mentioned, decision making is a big part of this job.

GOLDBERG: It sounds like you're describing the background of a Renaissance man.

BRADLEY: I hate to put it that way. When I was getting a master's in English, I heard someone say, "If you want to be a Renaissance man, you'll have to find a Renaissance duke who will hire you." I almost feel that that's happened to me, because I find that I'm able to function like that. I realize that sounds kind of ludicrous.

GOLDBERG: No, I think that's wonderful. That's a very hopeful statement for all those people who have a number of interests but feel badly because they're not focused on any one thing for a career. I'm hearing you say that all those interests can pay off—and in your case they did with a position as an editor.

Considering your experience, would you say that you need a college background to be an editor?

BRADLEY: I think so, because of the processes of handling information and the communication skills that are involved in the job. You need the kind of training and discipline that you can get from college and also the broad background in relating to people and using materials.

GOLDBERG: Can you generalize about the kind of degrees editors have?

WILSON: I haven't met an editor yet with an engineering degree, but an editor might have any kind of liberal arts degree: English, history, journalism, political science. People who have taken a wide range of humanities courses are usually well prepared for this kind of work, because they've learned to think and analyze and also to communicate effectively on paper. Of the journalists I know, a majority were not journalism majors.

GOLDBERG: Tell us how you found your jobs.

BRADLEY: I was program director of a statewide cultural organization, which was another position where I had to wear a few different hats. They had a quarterly publication and I worked very closely with the editor. She needed help occasionally, and when I was free, I worked with her. I basically had on-the-job training, and I found that there were things I needed to learn about the line-to-line work, but my basic judgment was solid and the versatility that I could bring to the job was a real plus.

GOLDBERG: So you learned to edit in that capacity. When you moved to your next job, was it in editing?

BRADLEY: Exactly.

GOLDBERG: Carol, how did you become an editor?

WILSON: I worked for six years on a daily newspaper, originally as a sportswriter and then as an editorial writer. It was a small city newspaper and I covered whatever had to be covered. It was good experience and when I moved to Madison, I found a job as a staff writer and moved pretty quickly to the editing slot.

But if I were to offer advice about what to do during college days, it would be to take advantage of whatever opportunities you have to write. And if an opportunity to edit presents itself, be it for a school newspaper or a literary magazine or a local paper, do it.

GOLDBERG: If you want to make a living as an editor, how can you find a job?

WILSON: You can always watch for advertised openings, of course. And libraries and placement offices have national directories of newsletters and other publications. It might behoove students who are really serious about editing to check those directories and see what exists in their fields of interest. Also, there may be professional organizations in their field or local agencies that do related work. People can explore what those organizations offer—they're likely to be producing written information of one sort or another. And of course, they can get in touch with the local newspaper.

GOLDBERG: Is it possible that people have areas of expertise that they don't code as such? Areas of knowledge that they could make use of in a newsletter?

WILSON: Yes. I think everybody has areas of expertise that they don't give themselves credit for. Too often we overlook the obvious and think that work has to be unpleasant. If it's something you enjoy doing, you convince yourself that you can't make any money at it. My first job as a sportswriter came about because I was a wild sports fan, and to this day, it was one of the best jobs I ever had.

GOLDBERG: Someone reading this might think that editing sounds just a little too good—that *everybody* must want to be an editor. Is it a very hard area to break into?

BRADLEY: I don't think so, but you can't have a narrow vision. If you've got an attitude of "anybody can do it and the jobs are tight," then sure, you've already talked yourself out of it. You have to be creative and flexible.

GOLDBERG: Would I be correct in assuming that any community of two thousand or more is likely to have an editor?

WILSON: Probably. That may be stretching it a little bit, but there is definitely material being edited for those people and there's likely to be a local newspaper in a community that size. There are *so* many small publications—in fact, it's said that if you wanted to find a newsletter for left-handed redheads who live west of the Mississippi, you probably could.

GOLDBERG: Let's say you have an interest in skiing and you also love words. Would it be possible to combine those interests in an editing job?

WILSON: I could see a couple of ways to pursue that. You might check to see what existing publications there are on skiing, including regional publications in states that have skiing resorts. You could send resumés to some of those publications. Then, while you watch for opportunities connected with skiing to open up, you can pursue editing locally.

A very good way to learn to edit is to find a job copy editing on a newspaper. You'll learn the precision of language, how to work under pressure, and how to work with people.

GOLDBERG: Do copy editors get paid better than minimum wage?

WILSON: Actually, copy editors are in some demand because more people want to be the *writer*, the *creator*. So newspapers let writers be paid in part by ego, by having their name on the by-line. Copy editors don't get ego payment, so they tend to make more money.

GOLDBERG: How much money might you make at your first editing job?

BRADLEY: Newspapers pay better than I think a lot of people would believe. Copy editors don't make such a bad living.

GOLDBERG: About $12,000 a year?

WILSON: In a small city, I would guess starting pay is about $10,000 or $12,000.

GOLDBERG: How about New York or Los Angeles?

WILSON: Maybe $15–20,000. A little less for a starting salary.

GOLDBERG: And how about upward mobility? If you start as a copy editor, where might you be four years later?

WILSON: On a newspaper, you might be a wire editor or editor of a section. You might be an assistant to a manager or a city editor. These are the kinds of steps you make along the way. It takes a while, especially on a larger newspaper, to get to the point where you have a major title such as managing editor, state editor, something like that. But a person with good copy editing skills has almost unlimited mobility within a newspaper. In terms of newsletters also, I would say there's a great deal of mobility.

GOLDBERG: I don't want to ask you what you make, but you seem to be at a middle level of upward mobility in the field. What might people in that range expect to make?

BRADLEY: It's common for people doing the kind of work I'm doing to be making $25–30,000. That's reasonable and attainable.

GOLDBERG: Do you think there will be more jobs available for editors in the next five or ten years, or fewer?

BRADLEY: My feeling is that there are going to be more. We're seeing decentralization of publishing in a sense. People are concerned about what's going on around them and I think they're responding to the regional publishers who have local interests and involvements. These publishers are starting to flex their muscles. So I think we'll find this portion of the industry, at least, stronger in the next ten years, and there will be more opportunities.

GOLDBERG: I've learned a lot from you and I'd like to try to summarize the main points. It probably takes a college degree to become an editor; a liberal arts background is just fine. Your training is best accomplished by writing, by working with as many publications as you can to build up your credentials and your skills, and by editing copy when you have the opportunity. There's currently such a proliferation of publications—newsletters, magazines, books, newspapers—that opportunities to edit are substantial. In fact, editing jobs are surprisingly available.

CHAPTER 12

Helping Professional

Detachment was one thing I learned about on my own. I really did believe when I first started this kind of work that a lot of people just needed a lot more love. And I think I've learned over the course of time that that's only one piece of the puzzle, and that if you love your clients like you love your brother, you sometimes find yourself in trouble.

—Judy Schector

JUDY SCHECTOR and STEVE LOWE are "helping professionals," a category that includes the remarkable variety of counselors and therapists practicing today. Neither Judy nor Steve has a degree directly related to their career, and although they warn that lack of a degree can limit options and earning potential, they identify several alternative avenues into the helping professions.

Steve started his own practice, specializing in primal therapy, in the mid-seventies. Judy works in the field of alcohol and other drug abuse. She counsels clients and teaches new staff members at Picada, an information and referral center.

GOLDBERG: I've always assumed that people have to have a graduate degree in social work or clinical psychology to get into the counseling fields, yet neither of you has those degrees. What's the story?

SCHECTOR: We have a lot of people with B.A.'s on the staff at Picada, and a couple of nurses, but it certainly isn't mandatory to have a master's. At other places I've worked, degrees aren't really a focus at all—what my degree is in hasn't even been a question on my interviews.

GOLDBERG: What kinds of places?

SCHECTOR: One of the places I worked was a residential treatment program for chronic drug abusers. When they recruit staff, I don't think their focus is at all degree oriented. In fact, a lot of staff people in the drug and alcohol field are recovered drug users themselves and are hired because of their experience, not because they have what are generally considered to be credentials.

GOLDBERG: They're ex-alcoholics or ex-drug addicts?

SCHECTOR: Yes.

GOLDBERG: Is that true across the country?

SCHECTOR: It's pretty traditional to hire recovered people in this field, and of course, some of those people are credentialed in the formal ways, but many aren't.

GOLDBERG: So, is the person who doesn't have a master's in social work or a drug-dependent background out of luck?

SCHECTOR: I have neither one of those and have still managed to work my way into the system. The network in the drug and alcohol field is very close and one of the ways I've managed to progress is by getting to know people in other agencies and being aware when a job is available.

GOLDBERG: Steve, you're a therapist with a master's in history. How did you do it?

LOWE: What really got me interested in becoming a therapist was my own psychotherapy. I had gone with my wife to the Primal Institute in Los Angeles. She wanted to take the training program and, essentially, I went along for the ride. I found, though, that once I got involved in the process, studying it and as a patient myself, I became hooked. I became convinced that this really was a method of helping people that could keep me working on myself the rest of my life and also provide me with a livelihood. My wife and I both practice primal therapy now, and I practice hypnotherapy, too.

GOLDBERG: So the credentials you offer your customers are . . .

LOWE: My experience. My personal experience, my having gone through the process first. I have a feeling that, for any kind of effective therapy, the best thing that you can bring to it is your personal experience of having really worked on yourself. By doing that, you can remain clear of your clients' problems to the extent that they don't hook you. You don't become argumentative or emotionally in-volved in a negative sense with what they're saying.

GOLDBERG: If you look at a psychology shelf in a bookstore, you'll see books about zillions of different kinds of therapy. Can you think of other kinds—besides primal—where people who have done some studying and have gone through the therapy process themselves can open a practice without the difficulties of a graduate degree and licensing?

LOWE: There's polarity therapy and there are people who are into astrological therapy. Of course there are a great many people who are not degreed in the holistic movement, including various as-pects of nutrition and vitamin therapy.

GOLDBERG: Judy, can you add to that list?

SCHECTOR: It seems to me what's most traditional in the alcohol and other drug world is what gets referred to as "confrontive ther-apy." It's based on the idea that when you're really direct with peo-ple, you help them come to their own understanding. I've been trained by some of my mentors to deal very directly, to pound on people, pound on their emotions and break down their images. It's much more direct than a lot of traditional therapy, but it seems to me that with people who have spent so much time avoiding their own persons, you really have to shatter their images to get any-where near their emotional state.

GOLDBERG: What I'm hearing from both of you is that formal training isn't as important to being a good therapist as who you are and what you've experienced and learned about yourself. But don't you need to have that Ph.D. in clinical psychology or a master's in social work when you're out there trying to get clients or a job?

SCHECTOR: There are certainly ways in which I'm limited by not having a master's degree. Were I to move across the country, where I don't know anybody, it might be harder for me to market myself. One of the advantages I have here in my own town is that I'm well known in the alcohol and other drug world.

GOLDBERG: What do you do at Picada?

SCHECTOR: A lot of educating in the community about alcohol and other drug dependency. That takes various forms, from very general to very specific one-on-one interactions. I might speak to a church group that's asked us to come and talk about alcohol or I might talk with individuals who come in and want to know whether or not they have a drug-dependency problem. We can help determine how much of a problem is related to chemical use and help find an appropriate treatment source.

GOLDBERG: Let's imagine the case of a person who says, "I know something about drugs and I know something about alcohol because I've had friends who've really been in trouble with both of them. I'd like to go into this field, but I really don't want to go through a degree program. I just want to get started and learn on the job." What would you recommend to this person?

SCHECTOR: That's a hard question to answer. I started at an agency geared to information and referral. It provided me with a lot of basic knowledge. It had a good library, and because people came seeking information, I built up a lot of knowledge about alcohol and other drugs.

GOLDBERG: How can people get hired if they don't have training or credentials? Is volunteer work one route?

SCHECTOR: Sure. That's always a good way to get a foot in the door. Volunteers at Picada often end up getting a job.

Another alternative, if you have enough self-confidence to promote yourself this way, might be to go to a treatment program and talk to the director. Just make an appointment and tell him or her, "I want to do this. When is your next job opening?"

GOLDBERG: Steve, do you have any suggestions for a person who wants to be a therapist and doesn't want to get retooled?

LOWE: I would say first involve yourself with the process as a client, so that you have an understanding of how it works from the inside. If you really derive benefit from it, you're going to have a source of motivational power that's much greater than if you simply read a book about it and hang up a shingle that says you're an X brand of therapist.

GOLDBERG: What if you want to go a more traditional route and not go into business for yourself?

LOWE: I have a feeling that would be very difficult. If an agency has the choice of hiring somebody who has a graduate degree in a related field, it's probably going to opt for that person, unless you are known personally.

GOLDBERG: And are there problems with being in business for yourself?

LOWE: Oh, yes. There is the problem of insurance coverage, for instance, and of course it's complicated now with the emerging HMO situation. That's one of several stumbling blocks, and in fact, after nine years of doing this without a degree that says "therapist," I've decided to return to the university. That will give me access to insurance coverage, to perhaps working part-time at a state or city agency. And also I would love to teach. I would love to teach at a university level, and except at certain alternative universities, you do need a degree to do that.

GOLDBERG: Do you sometimes feel like you're on the fringes of the mainstream without the degree?

SCHECTOR: Not so much within my field, but certainly with relation to other therapy models. What Steve was saying about insurance is true for me, too. I can't bill through insurance because I don't have a master's degree. Even though my experience is so much more than it would be if I'd gone to college for those years, the insurance companies need the degree. So that's a limitation, there's no doubt about it, and for that reason, it's easier for me to be involved in an agency than to be on my own.

GOLDBERG: And the pay is lower?

SCHECTOR: Right. I certainly don't make what I would if I were in private practice with a master's degree. But money hasn't been my driving force, otherwise I probably would have gotten a master's degree.

GOLDBERG: Steve, if you've become familiar with a therapy process and have gone through it yourself, how can you start a practice?

LOWE: For a start, I would make contact with various agencies within the community, including churches and educational institutions. I would volunteer to give lecture demonstrations. I would gain access to video or audio equipment and tape sample sessions. I would make myself known, make it known that I have something special to offer.

GOLDBERG: You've been doing this for how many years?

LOWE: It's been about nine years now.

GOLDBERG: Do you and your wife support yourselves from it?

LOWE: Yes, it's essentially our livelihood.

GOLDBERG: Do you work very hard, long hours?

LOWE: No, not really. In terms of session time per week, we each average maybe fifteen to twenty-five hours.

GOLDBERG: And how much do you charge?

LOWE: Thirty-six dollars an hour. I've compared our rates with other people at the master's level. Many of them in this town are charging about $60 an hour.

GOLDBERG: Judy, when you survey the various careers included in the helping professions, which ones could you get involved in without a specialized degree?

SCHECTOR: Just a basic information and referral kind of outfit, where people either come in or call to get information about services available in the community. I really enjoyed that kind of thing when I did it. You get lots of rewards because you're always helping people and you've got an answer for everybody who calls. I wish counseling were that easy and that fulfilling.

You could also start with some sort of educational process, teaching groups about some topic, like the teaching I do about alcohol. I find that very rewarding. People are usually there because they're interested in the topic, and it's also fun to be the expert in that kind of situation, and to be treated that way. I would also suggest looking into helping professions that seem less degree oriented than traditional therapy. Battered women shelters and rape crisis centers are female oriented and generally hire women. Incest is a big issue right now—and you can see trends. When I got my first job in this field, alcohol and other drugs was *the* issue, which meant there was a lot of public money in it and a lot of jobs were available. Battered women came after that, and incest is a big issue right now.

GOLDBERG: Tell us a little more about your jobs, your careers. Steve, what's it like to listen to people's problems twenty-five hours a week?

LOWE: Twenty-five hours is the upper limit for me to be effective. I think this would be true of any good therapist of any persuasion. It's very intense work and I even set up the day so that I don't have too many sessions in a row—maybe two in the morning and two or three later in the day, plus a couple of groups a week. If I go beyond that point, except temporarily, the quality of my work suffers, and so does the quality of my personal life. I need time, in a sense, to clear out my own stuff between sessions and just have fun. I'm amazed when I meet therapists who work eight- or nine-hour days, seeing client after client. That just wouldn't work for me.

GOLDBERG: Judy, you spend some time counseling people and some time giving information. What's good and bad about your day?

SCHECTOR: One of the things I like particularly about my job is that there's a lot of variety. I have a lot of different kinds of tasks and a lot of control over my workday in terms of what tasks I do when. I make a point of not doing any one thing too much in one day.

A bad day for me would be definitely a day that there's too much to do and not enough time to do it. I'm a planner by nature, and pretty good at not overloading myself. So a bad day for me is when I walk into the agency and someone says to me, "Judy, you have to do this today," and I wasn't planning on doing it. Fortunately, that doesn't happen too often.

GOLDBERG: Do you have a large client load?

SCHECTOR: No, although obviously that varies. A lot of people have problems during the holidays, so my client load is heavier then. And I find that when I deal with a lot of clients, I'll have so much empathy that I'll sometimes walk away feeling like I don't have the capacity to help.

GOLDBERG: Are you talking about burn-out?

SCHECTOR: I think so. Fortunately, I work with a lot of good people and if I walk out of my office feeling that way, I can turn to someone else on the staff and say, "I don't really feel like I helped that person," and get some help with that myself. We do a lot of that for one another, and I think it's very important. Al-Anon's concept about detachment is a good one for therapists when they're dealing with a lot of other people's problems.

GOLDBERG: What's Al-Anon?

SCHECTOR: Al-Anon is a self-help organization for people who are concerned about other people's alcohol problems. One of the things they suggest is learning to be a little detached. I think that also comes up if you go to school to become a therapist. You learn a little bit about the difference between you and your clients.

But detachment was one thing I learned about on my own. I really did believe when I first started this kind of work that a lot of people just needed a lot more love. And I think I've learned over the course of time that that's only one piece of the puzzle, and that if you love your clients like you love your brother, you sometimes find yourself in trouble.

GOLDBERG: Does that sound familiar to you, Steve?

LOWE: Yes, And also, there have been times when I've said, "Oh, my God, I just can't do this anymore. It doesn't work and I hate that so-and-so." Those feelings do come up, and I think they can be a real problem for anybody in this profession. For me, a little rest and processing of my own stuff will clear that away.

GOLDBERG: What question should you ask yourself before you enter this field?

SCHECTOR: You might ask, "But do I love myself?" I really think that the people who make the best therapists are the people who have a strong sense of themselves. It's not as though they're problem-free—I know very good therapists who have a lot of personal problems. But I do believe a strong sense of self is important in preventing burn-out, and a certain amount of toughness is important. You want to be involved with your clients, but you don't want to cross a certain line in the way you're involved.

LOWE: You also have to be graceful under fire, not be so affected by your own mood changes that the quality and consistency of your therapy suffers. You must be able to function day in and day out.

GOLDBERG: Judy, would you mind sharing with us what a person in your position—with several years of experience, but without certification—might expect to earn?

SCHECTOR: I'm guessing, but I think the average for the kind of agency I work for might be a starting salary of $15–20,000.

GOLDBERG: Without a degree?

SCHECTOR: Without a related degree. Many of the people that I work with have degrees, but like mine, they're quite unrelated. Sometimes you get a little credit for having a degree, and a little more money than you would if you have no degree at all.

When I first started working in this field, the first counseling job I had I started at $10,000. That was six years ago and that agency probably pays a little more now because of inflation, but I don't think you can expect to make much more than that without a master's when you start.

GOLDBERG: What's in your future? Where do you go from here?

SCHECTOR: That's a good question for me. Given that the thing I like most about my job is training other health professionals, if I move on, I'll probably move in that direction.

LOWE: I have a feeling that the issue of licensing for counselors might become increasingly thorny. There must be thirty or forty states right now that have bills pending before the legislature about licensing in the helping professions. And although I wish there was a way of keeping really unscrupulous people out of any field, I'm not convinced that licensing is the answer. There are a lot of wonderful helping professionals operating outside of the mainstream, without licenses or certification.

SCHECTOR: Even in the alcohol and other drug world, more and more states are requiring certification. In the job I do, it's not a requirement, but a lot of the people who do ongoing treatment of people with alcohol and other drug problems have certification.

GOLDBERG: Does that mean an advanced degree?

SCHECTOR: Not necessarily. Having a master's degree doesn't automatically make you certified. The basic requirement is that every year you get some training in some area. That's the way the states are going.

GOLDBERG: Is course work important in college? If you're not going to get a specific degree, is it still important to take courses?

SCHECTOR: This definitely expresses my own bias, but I would say that you'd probably do a lot better getting trained outside of the traditional university setting. An example in my field is the Johnson Institute, which is very well known and just does week-long and two-week-long training sessions. They're very highly thought of and if I were to look for a job and could say I was trained there, it would really mean something. It's more hands-on learning than college work tends to be.

GOLDBERG: In summary, you're describing a career that you both find personally rewarding and exciting, but you're also waving some warning flags. On the positive side, you're involved in careers that you believe in, that seem to let you keep some important values in focus. On the other hand, neither of you has made light of the problem of burn-out or the consequences of not being certified. Without credentials, your choice of direction is more limited, your earning potential is lower, you cannot bill through health insurance, and there are some likely problems ahead due to legislation governing certification of helping professionals.

CHAPTER 13

New Police Officer

I spent four years in the Marine Corps and there was a real closeness there, a camaraderie, because there was always the possibility that you'd be depending on the guy next to you for your life. I think the same thing exists here on the police force, but I didn't find it when I was a school principal. I didn't find it at all in education, that people are looking out for each other.

—*Pat Grady*

ALEX OLSON and PAT GRADY became police officers, in part, because of an attraction to the drama and action that are among its most publicized elements. Perhaps no other profession has been so fully—or so inaccurately—described by television and cinema. The actors and actresses who constitute the American media's police force are some of its most stereotyped heroes and femme fatales, with a few notable exceptions.

Alex and Pat dispel one stereotype right off the bat: both hold college degrees. Alex, who is a patrol officer, earned her bachelor's in art history from Smith College. Pat is a sergeant in his department and holds a master's in educational administration.

GOLDBERG: Alex, what led you to become a police officer?

OLSON: When I was six and lived in Cambridge, Massachusetts, my dad would walk me to school every morning. Way back then, there were traffic cops in the intersections, standing in little boxes that were actually out on the road. I'd see this cop every morning, directing traffic with a great smile on his face. He'd just use his lips and his fingers to whistle and you could hear his whistle three blocks away. To me he was a monumental, dashing figure. One day, wonder of wonders, he let me come out into the box and help him direct traffic. And that was when I was hooked.

GOLDBERG: How many years after college did you make the plunge?

OLSON: I graduated in 1969 and joined this department in 1981, so, eleven years later.

GOLDBERG: Why did you wait so long?

OLSON: After I graduated from college, I really had no interest in continuing in school and I wanted to give myself a lot of different job experiences. I wanted to see what the world had to offer and what I could do in it. I had a *lot* of different jobs during those eleven years. That was a really good experience and good preparation for what I'm doing now, and I wouldn't trade it for anything in the world.

GOLDBERG: Pat, you have a bachelor's degree in history and a master's degree in educational administration, and until four years ago, you were a high school principal. Why did you become a police officer?

GRADY: I'd been at my high school seven years and it was time for me to make some type of change, either become a superintendent in a smaller district or find another career. I had numerous friends in the police department and they talked to me about it and I thought, "Why not try it?"

GOLDBERG: What made you want to be a police officer?

GRADY: I think basically the action aspect. In a small school district like the one I worked in, you get to know all the kids, you go right down through the families. And I don't want to say it was boring, because it wasn't, but it started getting kind of old hat.

The police department offers a real opportunity for action. You're there when things happen, you're put on the spot a lot, and you're challenged. I like that.

GOLDBERG: Lots of people hold a stereotype that police officers are not college people, that the cop on the street is a high school graduate at best. Are you an aberration in that respect?

GRADY: No. More and more college graduates are going into this area, for several reasons. I think the action has something to do with it. Also, the pay in all the major cities and many of the smaller cities is very good and the benefits are excellent. And you meet a lot of nice people. If you work nights or if you work the three-to-eleven shift, you're going to run into some less savory people—more so the later it is in the evening—but the majority of the people you meet are very nice. And many of them have problems that you can help with. You can make a difference in their lives.

GOLDBERG: I understand from information your department gave me that in the last class of twenty-one new recruits, nineteen were college educated and most had advanced degrees. Is that typical of police departments around the country now?

OLSON: Police departments in general are upgrading standards of how officers relate to citizens and are changing the sorts of things that officers do. There's a trend to modernize policing, to be more aware of what the citizenry needs, and not just in terms of fighting crime. I'm sorry that so many shows on television imply that all we do is run around and have high-speed chases and shoot suspects full of holes, because police departments are becoming more concerned about social impact and about providing social types of services.

In that regard, people who've had a broader educational and employment background are going to be more apt to succeed than someone who's just had one job or a limited amount of schooling. And police work will be more attractive to them.

GOLDBERG: Do you think people might feel, if they've gone to all the trouble to get a bachelor's degree, that they're throwing it away if they join a police department, since it's not a requirement.

OLSON: It may not be required, but surprisingly enough there are things that I studied in art history that help me in this job. The ability to observe and retain my observations is a good example. I was trained to look at things and to notice little details and those skills are really invaluable to my work now as an officer.

GOLDBERG: What are your peers like?

GRADY: We have various types of people on the force, just like any other organization. We have people who are difficult to get along with and people who are easy to get along with. I couldn't generalize about them.

GOLDBERG: When you left your position as high school principal, you said one reason was a desire to move away from a bureaucratic position and to see more action. Did you get the action you were looking for?

GRADY: Yes. That and much more. Maybe 5 percent of our calls have something to do with a physical confrontation or even the possibility of a physical confrontation, but that 5 percent can be very difficult to deal with. I've been to stabbings, I've been to murders, I've been to very severe traffic accidents. These aren't situations that I particularly enjoy, but they can be very challenging.

GOLDBERG: Not boring.

GRADY: No, not boring at all.

GOLDBERG: Alex, can you tell us what a typical day, if there is such a thing, is like in the life of a patrol officer?

OLSON: I work the three-to-eleven P.M. shift. I get there about half an hour early, get into my uniform, get all my equipment together, and go into briefing.

GOLDBERG: What happens at briefing?

OLSON: Descriptions are given of stolen cars, wanted persons, missing persons. We'll be given new departmental memos, stuff like that.

Then I get my car and I check it out, make sure it's running right and equipped properly, and I drive it out to my assigned area for that day.

GOLDBERG: Do you have a partner?

OLSON: No, we have single-officer squads here.

GOLDBERG: What do you do then?

OLSON: I start patrolling the whole area in the car. If I get bored with that, I'll get out and walk around, and if I'm dispatched to a call, I'll go and deal with whatever it is. I may stop in at various businesses or other locations and talk to people to get information or just to say hello and find out what's going on.

GOLDBERG: Why would you do that? Why would you stop by for no particular reason?

OLSON: It makes good sense for me to become familiar with the area and it's good public relations to talk to people instead of just driving around in my car all day with the windows up.

GOLDBERG: Do you just walk into shops and say, "Hi. I'm Officer Olson. How are you?"

OLSON: Sure. I do that a lot, especially if I'm new in the area and they don't know me. I'll tell them that I'm the beat officer and if they have any problems they can call. Just so they know that there's someone out there who cares about them and is watching their store. It helps me to make personal contacts too, because then I know who the owner is, who's supposed to be there, where the doors are, all that kind of stuff that I need to know.

GOLDBERG: How much of your time are you just circulating and doing that kind of thing versus responding to specific needs?

OLSON: It changes from day to day. Some days I never have a chance to do anything but answer the calls. Other days I get one or two calls in eight hours and so I do a lot of self-motivated work. Just like any other job, it's good to be busy, have things to do, and there's a lot of action you can take on your own in police work. Everything from writing parking tickets to making traffic arrests to talking to shop owners.

GOLDBERG: Don't you hate writing tickets and having people hate you?

OLSON: It's part of the job.

GOLDBERG: Do you get a kick out of being on that side of it at all? Is there a certain power trip that's kind of fun?

OLSON: I won't deny that there's a lot of power and authority in this job, but I don't just stop speeders so I can laugh at them and say, "Ha ha, I got you!" I stop them because they broke the law that I'm empowered and duty-bound to enforce.

GOLDBERG: Would you describe some of the kinds of calls you get?

OLSON: All the things Pat mentioned. And I've been called to sexual assaults, suicides, neighbor troubles, husband-wife disputes. You name it.

GOLDBERG: And you go alone to these calls?

OLSON: It depends on the nature of the call. I'll be backed up by other officers if the problem is severe.

GOLDBERG: Suppose you get called to a stabbing. What do you do? What happens?

OLSON: There would probably be two or three other officers dispatched in a situation like that. We'd try to find out what happened, who the victim is, who the suspect is, if anybody saw it happen. We'd put the story together, search for evidence, protect the scene. There are a lot of steps to go through and a lot of it's common sense. A lot of it's also stuff that we studied at the academy, where we're trained specifically for each kind of incident.

GOLDBERG: How long was your training?

OLSON: Eight months.

GOLDBERG: How was that?

OLSON: It was very thorough and I think they did a really excellent job, but it got old hat toward the end.

GOLDBERG: Did you learn to be tough?

OLSON: No. I think I already was tough.

GOLDBERG: Physically?

OLSON: Yes. I had a job before I joined this department as a weight-lifting instructor, so I had a pretty good background in physical fitness. But we did study self-defense at the academy: about sixty hours of tae kwon do.

GOLDBERG: Have you ever used it?

OLSON: A couple of times.

GOLDBERG: On men?

OLSON: Yes.

GOLDBERG: Successfully?

OLSON: Yes. They went down.

GOLDBERG: Did they quit resisting at that point?

OLSON: One of them didn't.

GOLDBERG: And then what happened?

OLSON: We finally had two other people involved in making the arrest. So there were three of us all trying to control this one person.

GOLDBERG: Do you ever feel that, as a woman out there alone in a car, the risks might be more than you could handle? That a man might be able to handle them better?

OLSON: A lot of people have asked me that question. And the way you've phrased it, I'd have to answer no. But I do think that I know my physical limitations, and I'm not on a crusade to prove that I can beat everybody single-handedly. I think that would be stupid.

GOLDBERG: Pat, when you were on patrol—and I assume now that you're a sergeant you're not out there on patrol as much—how often did you have to be physical?

GRADY: Not very often. There were some instances when there was no choice, but for me and for most of our officers, being physical is probably the last resort.

GOLDBERG: Do you have to have a little cowboy in you for this job? A little bit of macho, just to keep your self-confidence where it needs to be?

GRADY: I don't think macho is the correct word. To me that means you're putting on a show and most people see through that.

Being in control is the right idea, knowing where you are, being yourself, and having confidence in yourself.

GOLDBERG: What's the worst part of your job?

OLSON: For me it's the disruption of my home life. That's been really hard to handle. When I first started, I worked nights, which is eleven P.M. to seven A.M. I'd sleep all day and I was a zombie when I was awake. After about four and a half months, I switched to the three-to-eleven shift and that's been a lot better, though it still causes a certain amount of disruption. I'm never home at night, I'm never there for dinner.

GOLDBERG: Do you have a family?

OLSON: Yes. I have two kids. I see them in the morning before they go to school and I often don't see them again until the next morning. And I really don't like that—it's a definite negative side for me.

GOLDBERG: Will that be a way of life as long as you stay on patrol?

OLSON: As far as I can see. I don't see any way out of it.

GOLDBERG: What about the day shift?

OLSON: I'd probably have to work twenty-five more years before I'd see days, because of the seniority system.

GOLDBERG: How about for you, Pat? Now that you're a sergeant are you removed from this problem?

GRADY: No, I still have the disruption. I just got off nights after seven months. Three to eleven, which is what I work now, is much better for me. And I work in the same area where I live, so I'm able to go home for dinner, which is nice.

I also have two kids and I miss things at school—soccer games and things like that. You always have to give up something, and in this job, the schedule can be a problem. And we're on a six/three work schedule, working six days, then three days off, so we get about every sixth weekend off. That's also kind of a drawback.

GOLDBERG: That does sound very disruptive. Is the divorce rate high on the police force?

GRADY: Yes.

OLSON: Nationally, it's one of the professions with the highest rate of divorce.

GOLDBERG: Do spouses worry about your safety the way they seem to on television?

GRADY: My wife worries, but I don't think it's a real continuing thing where it disrupts her life. I think she feels that I'm able to handle most potentially dangerous situations. We spend at least an hour or an hour and a half a day either running or lifting weights. I've had a lot of experience in self-defense. I use my head, try to avoid situations.

OLSON: Also, it's rare to intercept a situation just at the moment that the violence is occurring. Usually we're called after the fact, so that by the time we get there, nothing's going on, although the result of the violence may be lying there on the floor.

GOLDBERG: How much do you think about personal danger? Does that possibility keep your adrenaline up and make the job a high in a way? Or is it always a negative aspect hanging over your head?

OLSON: It's not negative. It keeps me on my toes all the time. I get worried when I feel myself letting my guard down or losing my concentration or starting to become apathetic.

GRADY: I spent four years in the Marine Corps and there was a real closeness there, a camaraderie, because there was always the possibility that you'd be depending on the guy next to you for your life. I think the same thing exists here on the police force, but I didn't find it when I was a school principal. I didn't find it at all in education, that people are looking out for each other.

If there's an emergency call, you get there as fast as you can and one reason is that the person who's in trouble might be you the next time. There's a real closeness on the street. Any personal animosity is left in the station for the most part.

GOLDBERG: Would you say, Alex, that there's bonding in police work that probably doesn't happen in other careers?

OLSON: Definitely. I've felt it since I've been in the department. I expected a certain amount of it, but I've been surprised at the extent to which it goes on. I think it's really good.

GOLDBERG: Is it fair to bill this interview and describe this career as the "new" police officer? Or is a police officer a police officer and always has been a police officer?

OLSON: I read an article recently that addressed that very question and described some changes that are taking place in police departments. There are many more women and many more racial minorities in police work nationwide than there used to be. A lot of departments have eliminated their height and weight requirements, or made them much less strict. Newer officers are younger and often have college degrees and a lot of varied life experiences.

GRADY: Also, most departments want people who can relate to their local populations. If your population is well educated, you're going to want officers who are well educated. In our particular community, that's the case. I think our officers need a college degree, I really do.

GOLDBERG: If someone starts today as a police officer, on this force or elsewhere, what might they make?

OLSON: Roughly $18–20,000.

GOLDBERG: Very good starting pay. And if they move up to sergeant?

GRADY: In my case, with the educational incentive, you're probably looking at $27–32,000.

GOLDBERG: So if you have a college degree, you get paid more than if you don't.

GRADY: Right.

GOLDBERG: Do you have any tips for those in college, taking liberal arts courses, who want to go into police work? How can they increase their chances of getting on the force?

GRADY: College students should get as much experience as they can in people-related areas. They can do volunteer work with alcoholics, with high school drop-outs, with people down on their luck. Those are the kinds of people and the kinds of situations that we deal with. Most problems we're called to help with are people problems.

Another good opportunity that most police departments offer is what's called the ride-along program. If you're eighteen or older, you can sign up and ride with a police officer for a shift. You can see what really happens and it can be enlightening.

GOLDBERG: How much of your job is social work?

OLSON: I was surprised at how much social work I was actually doing when I first hit the street.

GOLDBERG: What kinds of things?

OLSON: You name it. Talking people out of killing themselves, finding foster homes or temporary placement for abused or neglected children, providing transients with food and shelter for the night, taking drunks to detoxification programs, making sure that elderly people receive their Meals-on-Wheels.

GOLDBERG: Let's imagine two people. One has a strong social bent, a helping bent. The other has an enforcement bent; they like to keep people playing by the rules. If you have to choose one of those two, which will be happier as a police officer?

GRADY: I don't think you can choose one. You have to be adjustable and be able to deal with the situation as it is. If you can't do that, don't go into this field.

GOLDBERG: Let me summarize some of what you've said. Police work involves a lot of people work, a lot of social work, and many opportunities to use a broad educational background. The composition of police departments is changing: there are more women, more minorities, and more college-educated people in police work today than in previous years. It also offers variety, action, and a rare sense of support and community with co-workers. Two drawbacks were mentioned: the schedule, which can be very disruptive; and the danger, which, however real, adds an element of excitement to the job that is one of its attractions.

CHAPTER 14

Life Insurance Agent

I average about 175 dialings per week. That means times
trying to reach somebody on the telephone. And out of that
175 dialings, I reach about 50 people. Of the 50 people I
reach, I make appointments with about 15 to 20.
—*Barry Finkelstein*

JUDY JUNGEN and BARRY FINKELSTEIN came to life insurance
sales through extensive academic backgrounds. Judy has a
master's in American social and intellectual history and Barry
a master's and a Ph.D. in comparative literature. For both,
there was a period of disenchantment with the avenues opened
to them by their degrees, a skeptical first consideration of insurance sales as a profession, and eventually, considerable
pride in their success in the field and their genuine helpfulness
to their clients. They also express satisfaction with their earnings. Of all the professions discussed in this book, life insurance
sales probably offers the greatest possibility for financial rewards.

GOLDBERG: I think it would be useful if we started with a crash
course on life insurance and your role as agents.
FINKELSTEIN: Essentially, we sell two kinds of life insurance,
"term" and "whole life." There are many variations, but basically,
term insurance is protection only. It's typically intended to remain
in force until about age seventy, before the end of a person's life.
Life expectancy these days is mid- to late-seventies.
Whole life insurance is intended to remain in force until a person

dies. It charges a level premium, which initially is higher than what is needed to protect against death. And because it does, it creates what is known as a cash value, which can be used by the person in various ways before death.

GOLDBERG: Okay. Now where do you come in?

JUNGEN: We, as the salespeople, have to find people who are receptive to the idea of buying insurance. We call these people leads or prospects or referrals. I've been in the business ten years now and my new clients are almost all referrals.

I call these people and say, "Your friend mentioned that you may be interested in life insurance. I'd like to come and visit with you." We'll arrange an appointment and at that time, we'll talk about the problems and objectives that person may have as far as insurance is concerned. Then I go back and do my homework, look over that person's situation and various options. I fit the puzzle together and present it to him.

At this point, we may change our plans altogether or follow through on a basic plan. If he is receptive to the idea of purchasing insurance, he must be underwritten, which may mean having a medical exam and may mean answering questions about his company or his personal habits. We submit that information to our home office, which reviews it and eventually, we hope, issues a policy. We then deliver the policy to him and are paid a percentage of what he pays, his premium.

GOLDBERG: Is this like a lot of sales fields, where you're on the phone a great deal, trying to get a lead?

FINKELSTEIN: Not exactly. The lead is already obtained before getting on the phone. The phone call is a follow-up to having gotten the lead and having sent out a letter of introduction, so it's done to make appointments with people who have already been contacted.

GOLDBERG: A lot of people have an image of the life insurance salesperson as someone to avoid, and certainly as someone you wouldn't want to be, because you're always chasing your friends for business. Does that description offend you?

FINKELSTEIN: No. I think I had the same image myself before I went into the business. Many people do, and part of our job is to correct that image, to educate the public and give them an understanding of how we can be helpful to them. We find that a lot of the image problem is in the agent's own mind, and if it can be overcome there, it's relatively easy to overcome it in the client's mind.

GOLDBERG: Judy, could you describe a typical day in the life of a life insurance agent?

JUNGEN: I guess I have to begin with the very basic statement that there is no typical day. It's a completely unstructured day.

I usually start my morning with paper work, dictation, and review of updated or new material. I see clients about two to three hours a day and I end my day by returning phone calls and doing more paper work. My paper work is done in the office, but most of my appointments with clients take place out of the office, so I'm not confined. I very seldom have evening appointments. I spend evenings at home with my family.

GOLDBERG: Barry, is your day similar?

FINKELSTEIN: Like Judy, I have no typical day, and that's one of the virtues of the business. But my day is somewhat different from Judy's in that I do work at night, and I tend to do my paper work on the weekend, so that more of my day is spent making appointments and seeing people, both in the office and out.

GOLDBERG: You're both very successful in a tough field. Judy, you've been in this business for ten years and Barry, five and a half years. Can you tell us why, when many other people are failing as insurance agents, you are succeeding?

FINKELSTEIN: I work very hard. My typical week is in the area of sixty-five hours, including five evenings and one day on the weekend. I also came into the business with the understanding that I would have a great deal of changing to do in terms of my usual habits of behavior. My assumption was that if I listened to what I was told and studied on a continuous basis and worked very hard, I would have a shot at being successful in this business, and that's what I proceeded to do. In very brief terms, that's the reason I've been successful.

Also, selling was never something that appealed to me before going into insurance, nor was it something I did well, but I've also found, somewhat to my surprise, that I have a good sales personality.

GOLDBERG: I'm hearing you say you followed the rules, you were in effect a "good boy," and that's all you had to do for success. Somehow, I think there's got to be more to it.

FINKELSTEIN: What's happened over time is that I've developed my own style and gradually departed a little from the book, from the techniques described in the training programs. At this point, I can size up a prospect fairly quickly, have a good idea of what he's most likely to buy, and simply try to develop the presentation I'm making along those lines in fairly subtle ways.

GOLDBERG: Would you describe the training programs?

JUNGEN: Virtually all insurance companies hire people knowing that they have no experience, and they provide very valuable training at no cost to the prospective employee. And the continued training, for our company, is five years of weekly training sessions. I think this is where insurance companies really shine. I have no idea of its value, but it's a tremendous amount of sales and informational training.

Much of what's taught initially may involve licensing requirements, which vary from state to state. In Wisconsin, there's a basic test that you must pass before you can actually sell insurance.

FINKELSTEIN: My initial training program was two weeks long. It was very sales oriented and its purpose was to prepare me to go into the field and start selling. I'd done some self-study before to get ready for the licensing exam and I'd mastered the essentials of life and disability insurance.

However, as Judy mentioned, training is really a long-term process. I recently completed the Chartered Life Underwriter designation. That took me five years and that's sooner than most people do it. I'm working now on my National Consultant designation, and beyond that, I'll be working on the master's degree in financial services, which will be another five years of study. So the training is really a continuous, long-term proposition.

GOLDBERG: Much of that seems oriented toward consulting. When all is said and done, are life insurance agents salespeople or are they consultants?

JUNGEN: I think you have to be both. For the first year or two, you're developing technique, rapport, and sales ability. You don't have the experience or the expertise yet to go into the advanced areas, to really do consulting.

GOLDBERG: When people fail in this business, is it more likely to be because they don't grasp the sales techniques or because they don't grasp the academic aspects?

JUNGEN: I think it happens for two reasons, and lack of sales ability is one of them. There are a phenomenal number of beginning insurance agents who grasp the necessary knowledge but can't sell, can't deal with people on a very basic level. Second, as Barry said, the hard work is absolutely required and without it you won't succeed. This isn't an eight-to-five or a nine-to-five job.

GOLDBERG: How do you do the selling, Judy? How did you begin to find your customers?

JUNGEN: The standard way is to approach your friends. I did not do that. I decided that I wanted to work in a specific market, and that market was business owners. I began contacting people I thought might be interested in life and health and disability insurance, which were my basic lines. And I did face a lot of nos.

GOLDBERG: How did you find people to contact?

JUNGEN: I used various references: business directories, the Yellow Pages.

GOLDBERG: You're not saying you called strangers?

JUNGEN: Yes, I called strangers.

GOLDBERG: That's scary.

JUNGEN: It's scary, but you know, you really do it all the time anyway. You're constantly talking to strangers, whether it's the man who repairs your washing machine or the man who delivers your laundry.

GOLDBERG: How do you know how to talk to them, how to approach them so that they'd be interested in talking to you?

JUNGEN: As part of your training, your company furnishes you with what are called "sales tracks," sample conversations with prospective clients.

GOLDBERG: Suppose you call me and my response is, "You're from a life insurance company? I'm very busy. I don't need life insurance." What would your training tell you to do?

FINKELSTEIN: Essentially, we're told to try to get the appointment, not to get into an argument with prospects or try to sell them on an idea over the telephone. So my response would be, "I can appreciate that and I wasn't assuming that, just because I called you, you'd be in the market for life insurance. But I would like to have the opportunity to meet you, talk to you for a few minutes, and share some ideas and information with you that you might find useful."

GOLDBERG: When you started making those calls, did you believe deep in your heart that you had something important and worthwhile to offer?

JUNGEN: Absolutely. I was not going to waste my time on something I didn't feel was valuable for the person I was calling. I believed in it then and I do now and I don't think I've ever had a day when I didn't. I think that's a commitment we feel before we begin the career.

GOLDBERG: Did you feel it before you even went into your training program?

JUNGEN: Oh, yes. I did counseling of widows for a number of years and that convinced me of the value of life insurance.

GOLDBERG: Barry, do you agree that you have to believe in life insurance to be successful selling it?

FINKELSTEIN: I think the more you believe in it, the better you can do.

GOLDBERG: And before you got into the field, did you believe that life insurance was a positive thing?

FINKELSTEIN: Yes. I satisfied myself that the insurance industry had kept its promises to the American people for the past 150 years or so. I had confidence that it was an honorable institution and that it offered products I could feel comfortable selling. That it is a true service. That wasn't my main motivation for going into the field, but it was an important element in my being able to do it comfortably.

GOLDBERG: At this point in your career, how many people do you contact by phone in a week, and how many do you actually see face to face?

FINKELSTEIN: I keep careful track of that, so I can probably give you some pretty accurate numbers. I average about 175 dialings per week. That means times trying to reach somebody on the telephone. And out of that 175 dialings, I reach about 50 people. Of the 50 people that I reach, I make appointments with about 15 to 20.

GOLDBERG: And if you see fifteen or twenty people face to face each week, how many buy insurance?

FINKELSTEIN: I'm averaging three policies a week.

GOLDBERG: How do these numbers compare to yours, Judy?

JUNGEN: I maybe only make twenty-five phone contacts. I consider phone contacts someone who is there and answers me. Of the referrals, I probably see three-fourths in person. And I like to see ten to fifteen other prospects, business people, per week.

GOLDBERG: How do you get your referrals?

JUNGEN: Any client of mine might call with a name. And there are certain attorneys and accountants I've dealt with over the years who've brought me many customers.

GOLDBERG: Barry, how did you fare financially your first year in the business?

FINKELSTEIN: My gross income was $28,000; net was $22,000.

GOLDBERG: Judy?

JUNGEN: I think my gross income was a little more than that, about $30,000. And I netted maybe $27–28,000.

GOLDBERG: Barry, would you mind telling us how you're doing now?

FINKELSTEIN: Last year, which was my fifth year, I earned $83,000 gross. My net was $46–47,000.

GOLDBERG: In your tenth year, Judy, can you give us an idea of the range you're in? Have you hit the six-figure range?

JUNGEN: Almost.

GOLDBERG: Are those numbers typical in your field or are you exceptions to the rule?

JUNGEN: I don't consider myself the exception at all. As far as being typical, the first few years in the insurance industry are very difficult, but for people who can survive those, I think my income is average. There are people in our industry, people I know personally, who make four or five times what I make. Perhaps they're more talented than I, or work harder than I, or have been in the business twenty or thirty years.

GOLDBERG: How's your ranking compared to the other agents at your agency?

FINKELSTEIN: We have about seventy-five agents and I'm certainly in the top ten.

GOLDBERG: What do you think the average is?

FINKELSTEIN: Actually, kind of low. For the company as a whole, the average gross is about $50,000 and the net about $30,000.

JUNGEN: Ours is about the same, but we have to point out that first-year people are compounded into those averages. If you take out agents in their first two years, the grosses are much higher. It's those early people who pull down the average.

GOLDBERG: Do you love everything about selling insurance?

FINKELSTEIN: No. I'm still struggling to some extent with the uncertainty, despite the fact that I see my income continuing to grow. Until fairly recently, I've wondered whether I would continue to earn at the same level or higher. That's beginning to fade more and more as time goes on.

One thing that people must understand about insurance is that there's a very long time frame involved. To mature in this business takes many years.

GOLDBERG: What about the tremendously long hours?

FINKELSTEIN: I don't really think my hours are longer than that of most professionals. A lot of my clients are attorneys and I can't believe how hard they work. Some of them get into the office at six in the morning and work until eight or ten at night. Eighty hours is not an unusual workweek in the law field. Many of my clients are doctors, and they work enormously long hours, too.

JUNGEN: What's missing from what you're saying is that perhaps there are people who are more organized than other people. The long hours may be necessary for some and may not be for others. It's more accurate to focus on the really hard, dedicated work rather than the long hours.

I think my one reservation with this industry is the stress of needing to always be right. That's a very difficult thing to try to fulfill. You're trying to give your clients the most accurate advice possible at any one point in time. However, there is no *one* right answer in most client situations, and the industry is constantly changing. There are new ideas, new tax laws, new kinds of insurance, or wrinkles in the old.

GOLDBERG: Judy, is your background in social and intellectual history helpful in selling insurance?

JUNGEN: I suppose so. It doesn't seem obvious, but in that training you look at history in terms of thought patterns, thought movements, and social pressures as opposed to political events, and I think it has helped me to develop an awareness about what people are thinking or feeling. I can feel, perhaps, more what a client is not telling me than what he is telling me. That's very very helpful in a sales situation.

GOLDBERG: Barry, you have a master's and a Ph.D. in comparative literature. Is that background helpful in selling insurance?

FINKELSTEIN: Yes. Like an attorney, I've been trained to think. And the ability to think is very helpful in the sale of insurance.

GOLDBERG: In this business, what kind of person makes it and what kind of person doesn't?

FINKELSTEIN: The kind of person who makes it in this business is somebody who has courage, by which I mean the ability to persevere in the face of obstacles and the ability to deal with difficult situations and find solutions.

Along with that, and very similar to it, is simple determination and the ability to work very hard. Organizational skills are vital. And it's very important that you be pleasant, be somebody that people can like and trust. You must be flexible and adaptable, able to relate to a lot of different people without sacrificing your own identity and personality in the process.

GOLDBERG: That's quite a list of qualities. Do you want to scratch any of those or add any, Judy?

JUNGEN: No. That's a tremendous answer.

GOLDBERG: If a college student is interested in going into insurance sales, what courses would you suggest?

FINKELSTEIN: It would make sense to take courses in communication skills, psychology, speech, even acting. Also, courses in financially related fields, accounting, business, things of that sort.

JUNGEN: My number-one choice would be a very basic accounting course. The basic knowledge of how finances work, what those numbers mean on a statement, is incredibly important.

GOLDBERG: Finally, for someone who's decided to go into life insurance sales, how do you find the right agency? How do you land the right job?

FINKELSTEIN: First, it's relatively easy to get interviews with life insurance companies, because they're always looking for good people. However, as Judy pointed out, it's very expensive for them to train new agents, and only the major companies are taking on that responsibility and expense. So it would be a matter of finding one of those companies and contacting it.

JUNGEN: And if someone's in a small town and maybe there's only one agency system, fine. Go with that company and get the basic training. As you mature in your career, you can always make a company shift.

GOLDBERG: Any last words?

FINKELSTEIN: One of the key points to recognize is that we're not only offering a product, we're offering a service. You go to an attorney or a CPA when you're looking for somebody who has expertise in the field of law or the field of accounting. Part of our service is the counsel of a highly trained mind to deal with protection issues.

GOLDBERG: Let me summarize briefly. The life insurance agent can reap very substantial financial rewards, given a few requirements. From the outset, it is essential that the agent believe in the profession. Hard work is an absolute necessity and the financial compensation might not seem adequate for the first couple of years. An understanding of how to deal with people is essential, and however good your factual understanding of the field—and there's a lot to understand—you won't make it as an insurance agent without excellent person-to-person skills.

CHAPTER 15

Stockbroker

I saw a study recently in which people were asked to list ten
reasons why they stayed with their stockbroker. Making
money was either reason four or five, I don't recall which.
Reason number one was "My broker understands me, and
we have a rapport."

—Karen Wulff

STEVE WALLMAN and KAREN WULFF approach their careers as
stockbrokers with strikingly different styles. Both are in their
early thirties, both work for major brokerage firms, and both
are doing well financially for themselves and their clients. The
difference comes in the intensity of their commitments. Karen
readily describes herself as a workaholic and works fourteen-
hour days with some frequency. Steve prides himself on his
laid-back attitude and the fact that he leaves his office promptly
at 4:30 in the afternoon. Despite such different styles, both are
top brokers in their companies. Karen works for E. F. Hutton
and Steve for Merrill Lynch.

GOLDBERG: Karen, can you try to describe a typical day in the life
of a stockbroker?

WULFF: You bet. My day normally starts at about eight o'clock. I
get into the office and the first thing I do is look through all the news
wires. I peruse the *Wall Street Journal* and look at any news that's
come over our in-house system during the evening.

Calls from my clients start coming in within the first half hour.
After that, I'm busy talking with them and making buying and sell-

ing decisions until about one-thirty or two, when my markets close. I trade more commodities than stocks, and those markets close earlier. The rest of the afternoon is spent tying up the paper work and loose ends that I've created during the trading day. A lot of my late afternoons and evenings are spent in my clients' homes, on their farms, and in their places of business. Yes, that is a fourteen-hour day.

GOLDBERG: Is that really typical?

WULFF: I do that probably two to three days a week.

GOLDBERG: Let me ask right up front: are you a workaholic?

WULFF: Yes. I'm very much invested in being successful, as far as my self-image is concerned.

GOLDBERG: Steve, does that describe your work life?

WALLMAN: I think maybe the difference between us is that I absolutely never consider myself a workaholic. I like to try to be a little laid back.

GOLDBERG: Is your workday similar to Karen's?

WALLMAN: Yes. I basically read the paper until about a quarter to nine, dial and smile until three, and clean things up until about four-thirty.

GOLDBERG: And then you're done?

WALLMAN: Right.

GOLDBERG: Karen, how long have you been in the business?

WULFF: Two years.

GOLDBERG: Steve, how long have you been in the business?

WALLMAN: Three years.

GOLDBERG: This is a very difficult question so very early on in this discussion, but can we compare success?

WULFF: First, you have to ask what the measures of success are. The company rates us only in terms of gross commissions, but another kind of success is whether we make money for our clients. My gross commissions this year should hit about $85,000, of which I'll keep about 35 or 40 percent, depending on the product. Stocks are different from bonds in that respect, and bonds are different from commodities.

GOLDBERG: So you'll be making about $30,000 by the end of your second year?

WULFF: Yes.

GOLDBERG: And your first year?

WULFF: I made a comfortable living, but nothing like that.

GOLDBERG: Were you that successful after two years, Steve?

WALLMAN: Oh, yes.

GOLDBERG: How did you do it, with your laid-back style?

WALLMAN: I guess I like to work with people who appreciate that. Most of my clients, not all of them, of course, but most of them like to work with someone who's laid back. It's just a matter of finding enough clients who like my style to make a living.

GOLDBERG: Karen, you talked about being successful for your clients. First, can you give us a specific description of the things you're helping your clients buy and sell. What are all the different products?

WULFF: I deal almost exclusively in the markets, in the commodity market, the stock market, and the bond market. There are other products that brokerage firms sell, for example life insurance policies or tax shelter programs. These are limited partnerships generally involving either real estate or oil and gas exploration, and they're examples of nonmarket products.

GOLDBERG: That long list of specialized terms might already be enough to frighten away a potential stockbroker. If I decided to enter the field, could I be fairly sure I'd get the necessary training to understand it?

WULFF: Most certainly. You're taught all about it in the company training.

GOLDBERG: So do you get hired first and then learn about the work?

WALLMAN: You get hired and then you spend the first two or three months studying to take the licensing test. The license means that you are qualified, in terms of basic knowledge, to sell stocks. You know what they are, know how they're valued, and so on.

During the last month of the training program, you learn *how* to sell, *what* to sell, and how to utilize various resources within your firm.

GOLDBERG: Are you salaried during that period?

WALLMAN: You're salaried in some firms just during the first three months, while you're in the training program, and in other firms for as long as two years.

WULFF: It depends on the firm. They want to have you generating enough business to go from salary to commissions without really losing a step.

GOLDBERG: Is it hard to get hired by a brokerage firm?

WULFF: That depends on whether we're in the middle of a bull market or a bear market. I've heard from some of the old-timers that as the markets become less active, a lot of people drop out of the business. Since we're paid by our commissions, unless we're busy buying and selling and trading, our income will go down.

GOLDBERG: For those who may not know, a bull market means the stock market is going up, and a bear market that the market is going down. During a bear market, brokers are less popular, fewer people are calling them.

Then, is it easier to get a job with a brokerage firm in a bull market?

WULFF: No, I think it's easier in a bear market, because the existing brokers are dropping out, the attrition rate is higher, there are empty desks, in effect, empty space.

WALLMAN: I think anybody who's really going to make it as a broker should be able to get a job in a bear market or a bull market or any other kind of market. That's because the most important selling job you're ever going to have to do is the one that gets your foot in the door of the firm you want to work for. And if you can't sell yourself well enough to get the job, regardless of what the market is doing, then you probably don't have any business being a stockbroker.

GOLDBERG: You hit a buzz word there, Steve. You said that basically you're a salesman. I think that's going to surprise a lot of people who picture a stockbroker as being first and foremost a financial adviser.

WALLMAN: You want to be the wise adviser and you've got to be a successful investor. But the one criterion you *must* bring, the one criterion that you can't succeed without, is the ability to sell and sell well. We're basically salesmen and the company looks for selling background and selling skills when they hire new brokers.

GOLDBERG: How much does interest in investments have to do with one's success as a broker.

WALLMAN: Practically speaking, I'd say there's no correlation. I've seen stockbrokers who are not particularly absorbed by the markets do very very well. And I've seen brokers who are very interested in it do very well and I've seen the reverse of each. The key is, you have to be able to sell.

GOLDBERG: What does that mean? What are you selling?

WALLMAN: What you're basically trying to do is get someone to place their assets with the firm and allow you to suggest investments to them on an ongoing basis. Every time they agree with one of your ideas, every time they pick one up, you make a commission, and that's what pays the bills.

GOLDBERG: So selling for you means selling yourself to people, getting a stable of people who come to you to make and secure a transaction. And you need either a lot of people or a few people with a lot of money. Does that explain it?

WULFF: I think so. And I have a feeling that the longer you're in the business, the fewer clients you end up with, but those clients are more active, sophisticated, and well-to-do.

However, I think if you're going to last in the job, you really have to be in love with the markets and learn to understand them and make money for people. You see a lot of people who do well the first two years and then the third year you don't know where they are, they've disappeared.

GOLDBERG: And as I understand it, your commission is based on the dollar volume of trade, not the number of clients or the number of trades or the success of those trades. Which is it that satisfies your clients: the reality of whether you've made money for them or the appearance that you're doing as well as anybody else could have?

WULFF: That's an interesting point. I saw a study recently in which people were asked to list ten reasons why they stayed with their stockbroker. Making money was either reason four or five, I don't recall which. Reason number one was "My broker understands me, and we have a rapport."

GOLDBERG: This is very disillusioning. Don't you feel bad about the fact that this is really a sales profession more than an investment counseling profession?

WALLMAN: I think that's the biggest problem that people coming into the business have to come to grips with. Most of them figure they're going to be financial counselors, all that kind of thing. And the truth is, sales come first. Everything else is second to sales.

GOLDBERG: How do you find your clients?

WALLMAN: I try to initiate relationships, try to get people interested in me as a broker or me as an idea producer. I ask them to let me call from time to time with ideas. If I can do that, eventually they'll say, "Yeah, that idea sounds awfully good. Let's go with it."

GOLDBERG: How much time do you spend calling strangers, trying to get them interested in you?

WALLMAN: Never as much as I should. The cold calls are the toughest part of the job. Picking up the phone, calling a guy who you know has money, trying to get past the secretary, finally getting to him, and then not blowing it. And keeping your self-respect while you're doing that.

GOLDBERG: What happens when you reach that person? Do you ask him or her out to lunch?

WALLMAN: Generally not. I usually just ask if it's okay to call back with an idea from time to time, because all too often I don't have an idea at that moment, and I certainly don't have one that would be just right for this person.

GOLDBERG: And if one of these people says okay, then what?

WALLMAN: Then I try to build up that relationship. If someone invests in something I suggest, the success or failure of that investment will help to determine where the relationship goes. But I also keep the person apprised of what's going on and make new suggestions as ideas come up.

GOLDBERG: Karen, I have a feeling you have a different approach to sales.

WULFF: I do. If I market anything, I probably market myself. It's not completely different from what Steve is saying, but I spend a lot of time and energy putting myself out in front of the public. I do a lot of radio shows; I've been on television; I try to use as much press coverage as I can. I go to a lot of organization meetings: Wisconsin Corn Growers, Iowa County Cattlemen, homemakers clubs, that sort of thing.

GOLDBERG: I wonder if you could do the things you're describing if you weren't in love with what you're doing, if you didn't have a passion for it.

WULFF: I'm very addicted to the markets, and the commodities markets can be even more addicting than the stock markets, because they move much more quickly. You can't forget them for a couple of days and then come back to them; they'll have eaten you in the meantime.

I also like to speak publicly. I guess I'm a bit of a ham when I get up in front of a group.

GOLDBERG: What percent of your clients are a result of your public speaking versus your calling them directly?

WULFF: Over 50 percent. Probably closer to 75 percent.

GOLDBERG: It sounds like a way to get clients with perhaps more dignity than the cold call.

WULFF: I think that's probably the perception on the part of the salesperson. I'm not sure that the client necessarily feels that way.

GOLDBERG: Karen, you have a bachelor's degree in philosophy, with a minor in Asian studies. Was anything you learned in college helpful in your career as a broker?

WULFF: Not from a technical standpoint, no skill outside of the ability to think and reason.

GOLDBERG: Steve, your bachelor's degree is in theology. Any help?

WALLMAN: Absolutely. I think it's the best training in the world. The key to theology, and the key to philosophy, is learning to seeing the relationships between things, learning to think clearly.

GOLDBERG: So you're glad you went that route rather than getting a business degree?

WALLMAN: Absolutely. I don't have any regrets at all.

WULFF: I agree. If I went back to school it would be in philosophy.

GOLDBERG: No kidding!

WULFF: And for the same reason. If the degree does anything, it teaches the ability to think and reason.

GOLDBERG: Can you describe the type of person who becomes a stockbroker, if that's a fair question? Is there any particular type?

WALLMAN: No. All shapes and sizes.

WULFF: Our office is a diverse group of people, but I suppose the thing they have in common is that they are decisive. In order to be a stockbroker, you need that and you need to be a risk taker and a control taker.

GOLDBERG: What are the parts of your own personality that make you a successful stockbroker?

WULFF: The fact that I'm always at a dead run.

GOLDBERG: Steve?

WALLMAN: Probably the fact that I always swim upstream. I don't know why, but I always have that tendency, and the one place that you're rewarded for that is Wall Street.

GOLDBERG: Why?

WALLMAN: You really don't make money going with the crowd. You make money going contrary to the crowd in your investment decisions.

GOLDBERG: But you've already said that that's not really important. The stocks you choose aren't as important as your ability to win customers.

WALLMAN: It's important to me. For many brokers, it's not, but I put a lot of emphasis on the success that I've had in my investing.

GOLDBERG: You know, there's something that doesn't ring true about all this. You want to convey to clients your image as a wise investment counselor, but deep down you're thinking that's not really as important as just making them trust you and like you personally and feel that you're listening to them. Are you living with a certain kind of lie in this work?

WULFF: I've seen brokers do it.

GOLDBERG: Does it bother them?

WULFF: I guess I can't speak for them. In some cases, I've marveled that it doesn't bother them, or doesn't appear to bother them.

GOLDBERG: Does your firm care? Do the large firms look at your performance only in terms of commissions, or do they look to see how wise your decisions are?

WALLMAN: Performance first and wisdom second.

WULFF: Definitely. Your job depends on how many dollars you bring into the company.

GOLDBERG: You both have bachelor's degrees in fields that deal with values. Did you have trouble making this transition to a world that measures your success based on the dollars you bring in for the firm, not on how well you perform for the customer?

WALLMAN: I have a tough time with that. The biggest problem I had in adjusting, though, was from the humanities, where you're constantly emphasizing altruism and saying, "Money isn't important." I wanted to be an English professor, and I figured I'd be lucky to make $20,000 a year. To go out and have the potential to make two or three times that my first year in the business was a little difficult to rationalize and come to grips with.

GOLDBERG: Are you getting over that?

WALLMAN: Yes.

WULFF: It's a continuing problem for me, and I think every broker has to make his or her own decision about it. Mine has been to make sure that I'm making money for my clients, and that remains as important a goal as my own personal production. When I lose faith or get depressed or discouraged about those dual goals, I will go to some of the people who have been in the business for a long period of time and get some perspective.

The feeling that I get from talking to those people is that in the long run you *have* to make money for your clients, because if you don't, if nothing else, you'll always be looking for new equity, new dollars to work with. If you're constantly decreasing the equity that you have in your personal book of clients, you're not going to succeed. You're better off taking the equity you have and making it grow.

GOLDBERG: Karen, what do you like the very most about what you do?

WULFF: Being successful at it. You can be instantly gratified in this job, by a successful trade or by successful production: having a good month, a good week, a good day.

GOLDBERG: And you, Steve, what do you like most?

WALLMAN: That, and just finding a good stock, making money on it.

GOLDBERG: For yourself or for your customers?

WALLMAN: For everybody. I generally buy what my customers buy.

GOLDBERG: Anything you don't like?

WALLMAN: Probably the uniformity of every day, doing the same thing day after day.

WULFF: I hate the office politics, although actually, because we work on commission and are independent in that way, there's probably less of that for us than most other professions. Salaried workers have to report to their supervisors and I would guess that kind of situation sets up more difficult office relationships.

GOLDBERG: Do your firms push you to sell certain high-commission investments, regardless of whether they're best for your customers? Do you face that kind of conflict?

WALLMAN: The firm is always going to have things that they push. If you're with a good firm, a firm that I would work for, they're going to push it, but then they'll back off. They'll say, "Here are the reasons, here's why we hope you'll do it," but the final decision rests with the broker.

WULFF: I would agree. The trend right now is toward what they call special products, nonmarket-oriented products: life insurance, tax shelters, etc. The liability to the company is less in the special products. When you have individual brokers trading in account, if they make a mistake, buy instead of sell, buy a hundred instead of ten, whatever it may be, the liability to the firm can be tremendous. So, they would rather we look for money and then hand it over to a money manager or put it in a special product. But they don't insist.

GOLDBERG: Are there bigger commissions in those special products?

WULFF: Yes, for both the broker and the firm. But ultimately, so long as you're bringing commissions to the company, you can be your own person. You can write your own ticket.

GOLDBERG: What tips or advice do you have for people who are thinking of becoming stockbrokers?

WULFF: Get some sales experience. It's relatively easy to get a job selling insurance, for example, and if you prove that you can do that for a year or two, you are very very saleable.

WALLMAN: Get rid of any glamorous notions that you might have about the business. The fact is, we make a lot of money if we're good, but the glamor of picking stocks and manipulating the market and seeing your name in the newspaper as being a star investor—you're not going to have any of that.

GOLDBERG: And what kind of person should not go into this field?

WULFF: You have to want it very badly. There's a lot of stress in this job. You can make a lot of money quickly, but you can also lose it quickly. If you're not sure you're willing to put up with that, I don't think you ought to try it.

GOLDBERG: In summary, you're saying that as a stockbroker, you are first and foremost a salesperson and your number-one product is yourself. You have to be assertive and courageous in the risks you're willing to take; you have to be a take-charge kind of person. According to Karen, in the long run you have to love the markets. Steve says that's not necessary for success. But you agree that your clients' good fortune is personally important to you, although it doesn't directly affect your income. A sales background is probably the best preparation for a career as a stockbroker, and the rewards of the profession can include high income and the excitement of working in a field that many people find fascinating.

CHAPTER **16**

Fund Raiser

> The good fund raiser makes it very clear to the potential donor that there is a needs/benefit exchange. We need funds, but in return for your giving us those funds, we're going to provide you with certain benefits, certain quality services that you value enough to make a voluntary contribution.
> —*Ann Bitter*

ANN BITTER and BRAD HOLMES didn't intend to become fund raisers. Both were successful in other careers: Ann as a communications director at a state university and Brad as a therapist. In both cases, when they were asked to apply for fund-raising jobs, they had the same reaction: "Fund raising? Me?" In hindsight, they can identify the skills and experiences that qualified them for this growing field and that have led to their present success. Ann is the director of development for a public television station, a station that receives half of its funding through private support. Brad is an assistant development director at a full-service hospital.

GOLDBERG: What kinds of organizations hire fund raisers? Ann, can you give me an overview?

BITTER: That's not hard to do because the number is increasing so rapidly. The list includes fields that are growing quickly, such as health care, and organizations that have experienced federal cutbacks, leaving them in dire need of funds. Arts and social service organizations are in this category.

HOLMES: Religious organizations have traditionally been very

167

strong and successful fund raisers, and I'm finding that more and more churches are hiring development consultants now, and so are universities and colleges. The American Cancer Society and the Leukemia Society and United Cerebral Palsy have all developed very strong fund-raising campaigns. Because of the budget cuts that nonprofit organizations have experienced, more and more of them are hiring fund raisers.

GOLDBERG: The key word seems to be *nonprofit*. I take it fund raisers work exclusively for nonprofit organizations.

BITTER: That's correct.

GOLDBERG: And is it safe to say that almost any large nonprofit organization would have use for a fund raiser?

BITTER: Absolutely. The larger the budget of an organization, and the larger its fiscal responsibility, the greater its need for someone to maintain funding and secure additional funding.

GOLDBERG: Could you describe in a sentence what you do?

BITTER: My position involves planning and organization and matching the station's needs to a financial plan for growth.

GOLDBERG: That sounds as if you develop a formal and precise program, but I think a lot of people's image of a fund raiser is someone who begs for money. Is that a label you have to deal with much?

HOLMES: I get that a lot, and sometimes it can be tough. I always kid people who know I'm a fund raiser. I say they have their hands in their pockets, holding onto their money, when I come around. When I tell people who don't know me that I'm a fund raiser, they look like they're not exactly sure what that means.

It's very difficult to explain the science and the techniques of what a fund raiser does in a sentence or two. The traditional view of a fund raiser is someone asking for money for a cause, coming door to door like in the old March of Dimes campaigns. But in the seventies and eighties, the whole field really changed.

GOLDBERG: How do you convince people to part with their money?

BITTER: The good fund raiser makes it very clear to the potential donor that there is a needs/benefit exchange. We need funds, but in return for giving us those funds, we're going to provide you with certain benefits. In the case of public television, it's quality programing. In the case of, say, a small theater, if you don't give us money, our shows don't get produced. We very definitely have to position ourselves as providing people with certain quality services that they value enough to make a voluntary contribution.

HOLMES: People give for a variety of reasons and one reason is recognition. It may be that they like having their name in print, saying that they helped underwrite public television or purchase a major piece of medical equipment. Sometimes people give to the health care industry because a certain piece of equipment saved somebody's life, or *could* have saved somebody's life if the hospital *had* owned it. Part of being a development director is learning to understand the psychology of giving. Understanding what motivates people to give is really a secret to being a successful fund raiser, and if you can tap their emotions and get them to become repeat donors, that's a real key to success.

BITTER: I'd add one thing to that and say that I think it's very important that you associate yourself with an organization that you can be personally proud of, because that's really where you derive your stature, not from a generic "I am a fund raiser."

If you ask me what I do, I can say with great pride that I work for WHA-TV. That instantly provokes a positive response because of my pride and because of the way the station's perceived in this community. I can then go on to make the next logical statement, which is, "I help to secure funding for that organization." And people respond by saying, "Oh, that's so important. Isn't it good that someone's doing that?"

My belief in the organization I work for is the reason for my success, and I know I couldn't do it for every organization. I wouldn't be very good in some settings.

GOLDBERG: To my knowledge, schools don't offer degrees in fund raising. I'm curious to know how you got started in this field.

BITTER: The first fund-raising job that I had grew out of a very different kind of a job. I had been working for seven years as a communications director in the college of engineering at a state university. In that position, I found that I needed to motivate people to provide us with various kinds of support, including financial support. So that was something I developed.

When a fund-raising position opened up at the college of engineering, I was asked to apply for the job. And when I protested and said, "But I don't know anything about fund raising," I was told by a person who's had years and years of experience that the only way you learn about fund raising is to do it. You need on-the-job training and you need help from people in the field who will take the time to teach you how to do it right.

GOLDBERG: Why did they ask you to do this?

BITTER: First, I had a knowledge of my subject area, the college of engineering. Second, and of equal importance, my skills in communication were very good. That is something that is absolutely critical in this field. You have to be able to articulate the value of an institution verbally and in writing.

HOLMES: I think the other important ingredient is creativity. The more creative you are, the higher your chances of successful fund raising. Because people are inundated with so many requests from so many deserving institutions, it takes a really creative campaign to stand out and get a response.

GOLDBERG: How did you get involved in fund raising, Brad?

HOLMES: I was in a completely different field, working as a therapist, and at the same time I became involved with a nonprofit organization. Funds were low there and we knew we needed to raise money. I decided we could do it by sponsoring a spaghetti dinner. We did, and it was an incredible success. I liked doing it and I got a lot of positive feedback for doing it. That's how I got involved in fund raising!

GOLDBERG: Why did you like the process so much?

HOLMES: I like dealing with people, and working with the public, and I found that it's really gratifying when I can influence people to give money to a cause that I believe in, through a letter I write or a special event I plan. And the special events themselves are really fun. They often don't raise the larger dollars, but they can have a hidden impact, because they'll cause people to remember the name of the organization in the future.

GOLDBERG: And how did you move from there to being employed as a fund raiser?

HOLMES: From there, I volunteered to raise money for a hospital. After I'd been doing that for about a year, one day the president of the hospital called and said, "We realize that development is something this hospital is going to continue to need. How would you like to start a program?" And I had the same kind of reaction that Ann did: "What's fund raising?" I'd raised money for them, but I didn't know what the "schoolbook" techniques were. That was in 1980, and that's when I made my career switch. And I've found it a fascinating field.

GOLDBERG: Your position now, Brad, is assistant director of development for a fairly large hospital. What do you do all day? Is most of your time spent sitting in a box all by yourself, thinking, "How can I raise money?" Or is it spent talking to people at the hospital? Or is it spent filling out government forms?

HOLMES: Thank goodness, I don't have a lot of government forms to fill out. Much of my day is spent in meetings, and I make presentations to various organizations, asking for their support. A few hours a day might be spent at my desk, thinking and planning. I compose fund-raising letters for direct mail and I plan special events. I may spend half of my day at my office.

GOLDBERG: How about your day, Ann?

BITTER: It's really very much like Brad's. I also spend a lot of time in meetings, and I guess I would put that under the heading of either taking advantage of or creating opportunities for a revenue stream.

One thing I'd emphasize about how I spend my day is that I try to have a lot of contact with potential donors. I think one of the biggest mistakes for a fund raiser is not getting out and seeing people. The professionals I know in the field who are least satisfied with their jobs are those people who are chained to their desks. You *have* to communicate with people in this job. You can have the best plan in the world, but unless you go out and actually talk to people one-on-one or write that direct mail piece and sent it out—that's another form of communication—you won't succeed. I think the highest failure rate in this business is with people who are good planners but poor executors.

GOLDBERG: You've given us another component of a successful fund raiser: a hands-on personality.

BITTER: Yes.

HOLMES: Absolutely. One of the most important qualities I see for a fund raiser is that he or she is not afraid to go out and ask for money.

BITTER: It's hard to take rejection and a good fund raiser has to be prepared to take constant rejection and learn not to take it personally. And it's important for fund raisers to realize that if they're working for an organization that is not perceived positively, then their job is not to get discouraged and give up, but to develop a marketing plan that enhances the organization's image and build from there.

GOLDBERG: That's a big job.

BITTER: It's a very big job, and the organizations that most need help and most need money have to take that step first or they won't succeed.

GOLDBERG: What's the best part of your job?

HOLMES: It's fun for me to write a creative letter and see a greater percentage of direct mail return than the national average. If the national average runs around 3 percent on direct mail, and I get a return of 5 or 6 or 7 percent, that means that something is sparking. Special events are fun for me, because I get personally involved in planning and running them. And receiving a very large donation is probably the ultimate.

GOLDBERG: You're saying that the biggest rewards for you are the goal achievements. Is the same thing true for you, Ann?

BITTER: Yes. I'm a very goal-oriented person and I love the challenge and the puzzle of trying to collect resources where maybe there weren't any before. I love that challenge. If someone said to me, you have to raise a million dollars in the next six months, I would try to rise to the occasion and not be faint of heart. I think that basic love of a challenge is essential in this work.

GOLDBERG: What are the different avenues you follow to get funds for public TV?

BITTER: The primary component is the membership drive, but we're finding that membership drives are not perceived quite as positively as they used to be by the TV-watching public. So, we're having to come up with new avenues of support, such as planned giving, which means giving a potential donor the opportunity to leave a certain portion of money to our organization in his or her will. We also do program underwriting and we have a large televised auction. Obviously, we try to associate everything we do with television in some way or another.

We raise $3.6 million annually in support of our station. That's about half of the station's total budget, and it's grown to be an enormous responsibility. Even the slightest decline in any one of the areas I've mentioned would have a very significant impact on the station's health. So we're always trying to be creative and find new ways to ask people for support.

GOLDBERG: I'm wondering as I listen to you how different your job is from what a salesperson does.

BITTER: We have a lot in common. In fact, fund-raising seminars have begun bringing in sales trainers. As people's discretionary income has become more and more limited in recent years, the competition for funds has become stiffer. That means you have to take a much harder sales approach than in years past.

GOLDBERG: Ann, if you were offered a job as head of a sales division at IBM at double the salary you're making now, would you take it? And would somebody in that position want your job?

BITTER: I don't think that a salesperson from IBM would want to have my job, because I'm not compensated as well for my efforts. And I think there's a very good reason for it. Fund raising is a very young profession. We're just now learning the techniques that salespeople have applied very profitably to businesses for years. I doubt IBM would come to me, because I don't think I've acquired the kind of expertise you need to have to sell a product. I'm getting there, but the reason I'm getting there is because I'm learning from professional salespeople.

GOLDBERG: Are you saying that this is a second-rate career compared to being in sales for corporations?

BITTER: No. I'm definitely not saying that. In fact, I would add to what I just said that I personally feel the need to associate myself with an organization that makes a contribution to the quality of somebody's life. You could safely say that about most nonprofits. Whether it's the humane society or a hospital or a public television station, it exists for the greater public good. I'm willing to accept a lower salary for that reason now, and I think the salary level for fund raisers is going to change gradually. The compensation levels will rise as the professionals themselves improve.

GOLDBERG: How about for you, Brad? Why are you working for nonprofits when there are bigger bucks working in sales for corporations?

HOLMES: I think it's because of the desire to be part of a program that I believe in. There's no doubt that you can make more money in industry right now, but I agree with Ann: fund raising is an up-and-coming profession.

Also, I'm here because I enjoy working with people. That's a big part of this job and I really like it.

BITTER: So do I.

GOLDBERG: What *don't* you like about being a fund raiser?

HOLMES: The hard part for me is sitting down and doing all the necessary technical work. I wish I had an accountant full-time who would do that for me.

BITTER: I think a negative part of fund raising is the long hours. It's a necessary part of the business and usually the extra hours at a special event or a function are enjoyable, but it does take time away from your personal life. You have to make a decision about just how far you're willing to go in that respect.

There's also very high stress in this job, and I think that's one reason why the profession has a high turnover rate. They say that the average fund raiser stays in his or her job only one to three years, and I think stress is one of the major reasons.

GOLDBERG: How can somebody get that first leg into the fund-raising field?

HOLMES: Volunteering is an excellent route. When I was volunteering, I learned a tremendous amount.

GOLDBERG: Brad, you have two degrees in psychology, and Ann, you have a degree in English. Is your college education helpful in your jobs?

HOLMES: Most definitely for me. Working with people is the greatest part of my job responsibilities. Ninety percent of the people I work with are volunteers, and I have to be sensitive to their personalities and their needs. Also, my background gives me a foothold into understanding the psychology of giving, and that's been very helpful.

GOLDBERG: How about your English degree, Ann?

BITTER: I'm a little more cynical about it. I did learn general communication skills, how to think and how to reason and interact with people. I think that's what a college education is all about and I think you do need a degree to get your foot in the door for any job. But I don't necessarily think that my English degree prepared me for some of the skills that are part of this job.

I can remember specifically the horror that struck me the first day I sat down to write a business letter, when I realized that I didn't know how! It hadn't been part of my training. I had to learn that kind of thing on the job.

GOLDBERG: What would you suggest for a college student who might want to go into fund raising?

HOLMES: I think business courses are very important and I've taken a number of them since college. I'd also suggest marketing courses, writing courses, maybe a business correspondence course.

BITTER: It's important that you have budgeting and accounting and management skills. There are also many fund-raising workshops being offered that provide an enormous amount of background information.

GOLDBERG: Let's talk about money. How well might you be paid if you've been in the field for, say, two or three years?

HOLMES: A starting salary for a director of development is likely to be $28–30,000. An assistant director or development associate might be looking more in the $20,000 range. That will vary a lot, though, depending on the location and the particular organization.

GOLDBERG: You've said that fund-raising positions are abundant right now. Are there going to be more or fewer fund raisers ten years from now?

HOLMES: I think there are going to be more opportunities in this field for proven fund-raising professionals. Unfortunately, there's the fear that a lot of organizations that have not had fund-raising programs are not going to survive the eighties. Hospitals and the health care industry are a particular concern because of their rising costs. How effective are they going to be in raising money? That's a real key to their survival.

BITTER: It does help the fund raiser to specialize. I think it's a good idea to start out as a generalist, decide what area you want to specialize in, and really concentrate on that area.

HOLMES: Larger organizations tend to have positions for specialists. They may have an executive director, an annual giving director, and a special events coordinator. Sometimes they'll have a marketing person or a writer specifically for fund raising. There are lots of opportunities.

GOLDBERG: Let me summarize some of this information. To be an effective fund raiser, you need to be a good communicator, both in writing and verbally. It helps to be creative and to be comfortable dealing face-to-face with lots of people. You probably need a college degree, and though it doesn't have to be in business, it helps to have had some business and marketing courses. Even so, you will probably do lots of on-the-job learning. Overall the career has a lot of pressures, a lot of rewards, and a lot of challenges.

CHAPTER 17

Small Business Owner

For me, working has actually been the easiest part. It was some of those early days when I just sat there all dressed up with no place to go that got me down. I'd think, "My gosh, if there was a customer here, I'd be so much happier. What can I do about that?" And the answer was probably, "Nothing, except hope and keep doing what you're doing and have faith in what you're doing."

—*Victor Mondray*

CAROL SCHROEDER and VICTOR MONDRAY own small retail stores. Victor, who holds a bachelor's in general science and is a former medical student, is the sole proprietor of Victor's Coffee and Tea, an establishment that sells gourmet coffees, teas, and accessories. Carol has a bachelor's in Danish and a master's in Scandinavian studies. She and her husband, Dean, own Orange Tree Imports, a shop that specializes in cards, gifts, and gourmet kitchen wares. Both stores are beautifully designed, bountifully stocked, and enticingly promoted. In short, they are examples of flourishing small businesses.

GOLDBERG: Victor, I've got to ask how and why you went from medical school to the retail coffee business?

MONDRAY: I was miserable being a medical student and miserable looking for a decent job after I quit school. I knew I didn't want to be one of those people who comes home every night and says, "Thank God, I'm home. I really hated the day; now I have to have fun to make up for it." For me, that was the impetus.

I'd seen nice coffee stores in other cities, in Boston and in New York, and I thought, "Gee, that looks like fun." I did quite a bit of investigating, talking with the owners of those shops, and it still sounded like fun. I think if you can investigate an idea and not get too discouraged, it's a very good sign.

GOLDBERG: Did you know a lot about business?

MONDRAY: No, but I have common sense, and I think that can get you a long way in the beginning. And the shop owners I talked to were very very friendly and helpful. They gave me a lot of good information and a lot of insights.

GOLDBERG: It sounds like you've given the concept of informational interviewing a new twist by applying it to small business. Carol, did you talk to people in the gift shop business before you opened your store?

SCHROEDER: No, but I think that's a good idea if you can do it. I guess I'm a little shyer than Victor. I go into stores and look them over pretty carefully, but I'd be a little hesitant to approach the owner and say, "I'm going to start a store. Tell me what you know."

I've always visited shops. That's something I've done since long before I planned to open my own. When I was studying for my degree, I was in Copenhagen for a year and I spent a lot of time looking at shops there. I really found the design level in Scandinavia inspiring, and I was intrigued by the thought that I might someday be able to create a Danish sort of shop in this country.

GOLDBERG: Other than looking at shops and talking to shop owners, how can you learn about opening and running a store?

SCHROEDER: Certainly by working in one. I think Victor was brave to open his own store without, I assume, any retail experience.

MONDRAY: That's correct.

SCHROEDER: And I didn't have much retail experience, but I had six months, which counts for something.

GOLDBERG: Working in a similar kind of store?

SCHROEDER: Actually working in the same store. I was hired as manager when it was a Scandinavian furniture and accessories store. Six months later, my husband and I bought it and changed its nature fairly extensively. Those six months gave me a chance to get my feet wet.

GOLDBERG: I take it neither of you took accounting or marketing courses before you opened your businesses?

SCHROEDER: No, but it would have been a good idea.

MONDRAY: When I dropped out of medical school I took an introductory accounting class and a computer programing class. I didn't really do it because I was opening my own business, but I would strongly recommend it.

GOLDBERG: The computer course too?

MONDRAY: The accounting course a lot more.

SCHROEDER: I still haven't had an accounting course. Being female and having decided in first grade that I was going to be a writer, I assumed that numbers were not going to play a large part in my world. Consequently, I didn't pay a lot of attention to math in school. I do a lot with numbers now, and it would be nice to have stronger math skills.

GOLDBERG: Let's talk about the opening of your businesses. Victor, you've told us that you did some research about coffees and equipment and so on. Did you try to predict the cost of opening the business and project sales and expenses and so on?

MONDRAY: I did as much as I thought I could. You can analyze a business in Chicago, where there's a base of several million people, but if you move that business to Madison, Wisconsin, which has a base of two hundred thousand, you can't expect your projections to be entirely accurate. I think the best you can do is an educated guess.

Of all the numbers and details and statistics that I looked at, there was one that convinced me that it was worth trying. The average American consumes 11 pounds of coffee a year. That told me that about 30,000 pounds of coffee are sold every week in Madison. From the projections I'd glued together, it seemed that a break-even point for my business was about 400 or 500 pounds a week. It didn't seem unreasonable to me that I'd sell 500 pounds out of 30,000.

I knew what the average mark-up in town was on gourmet coffee and I also knew that if someone came in for a pound of coffee, they might need some filters or maybe a coffee mug, too. So, I deduced an average transaction of a certain amount. Then it was just a matter of calculating how much was needed for rent and labor and other expenses.

GOLDBERG: Can you calculate those figures with any accuracy?

MONDRAY: Yes, some of them can be very concrete. If you have a location in mind, you can look at the real estate ads in the newspapers and see the rental cost per square foot in that area. And with salaries, there's no secret. Forty hours a week will cost you a certain amount, whether it's your time or someone else's. And you have to figure phone bills and advertising and so on. You can get an idea about those costs from almost anyone who has a business or from an accountant or even a banker.

GOLDBERG: Carol, is it as simple as Victor's making it sound?

SCHROEDER: There's a real limit to what you can project beforehand, and I think there's no question that opening a small business involves risk. It's important to know that and not to risk more than you can afford to lose. If you can't cover the rent or salaries or if you end up defaulting on your loan, what would it mean to you?

I recently spoke with someone whose father opened a small delicatessen two years ago and is now about to go bankrupt. He'll lose his house, his car, probably most of what he's worked for during his lifetime. I hope that when he went into business, he said to himself, "I'm willing to take these risks in order to try this." If not, or if, perhaps, his wife was not willing to risk losing their home, then I think the bankruptcy is going to be that much more devastating.

GOLDBERG: I think people should know the fact that four out of five businesses do fail within a fairly short period of time.

SCHROEDER: It's said that inadequate financial planning and undercapitalization are the two key factors to financial failure of small businesses. If you don't have enough money to make it through that first year or if you don't have enough inventory to interest the public, that can cause failure, too. But I think that the unseen factor in some of those failures is that people sometimes don't find running a business as pleasurable as they expected or they find that their spouse isn't supportive enough.

GOLDBERG: When you bought your business, how large was it in terms of sales and size of the store?

SCHROEDER: At that time, the store was 1,000 square feet, which is quite small.

GOLDBERG: About the size of a big two-bedroom apartment.

SCHROEDER: And we had very little storage space. Since the store had only been in operation six months, it was hard to say what the annual sales would be, but our goal for the first year was $50–100,000 in sales.

GOLDBERG: And how big, how valuable, was the inventory?

SCHROEDER: I think about $7,000.

GOLDBERG: How much cash did it take to buy the business?

SCHROEDER: We started with about $8,000 of our own, which was used partly as collateral for a bank loan and partly to finance the purchase of the business. And our initial bank loan was about $12,000, I believe. I would say you'd have to have at least $50,000 to start a comparable business today. That would be a total, including the bank loan.

GOLDBERG: How much money did you start with, Victor?

MONDRAY: I was lucky. I started with $20,000, which was loaned to me by my parents. Without a proven track record and without a lot of assets to use as collateral, it's hard to get a bank to give you money. Once you're established, it's much much easier, but I can guarantee that the first time will be hard.

So, it took $20,000 for me to start, and my store was only 500 square feet.

GOLDBERG: Did you borrow additional money, or just the $20,000 from your parents?

MONDRAY: Actually, they loaned me $10,000 and cosigned a $10,000 loan. And if we hadn't had good sales from the first day, we would have had to borrow more in a month.

I might also mention that when I opened my store, I was single and had relatively few obligations. That was really a big factor. If I'd had a wife and a couple of hungry children at home, I don't know whether I'd have had the gumption to do it.

SCHROEDER: My situation was similar. My husband kept his job for the first two years that we had the business, which meant that I wasn't the sole breadwinner and the business didn't have to carry the burden of a spouse and children and a home. Those kinds of expenses can be very hard to meet, especially during those first few years. We always paid ourselves a salary, but for many years, we put most of our money back into the business, which is what allowed it to grow.

GOLDBERG: There's a basic difference in your situations. Carol, your shop already existed, and it's not that hard to imagine analyzing and changing an existing business. But Victor, you created a business from thin air. Any thoughts about that?

MONDRAY: I think with a small business, it's really helpful if the excitement comes from inside of you. If you have a lot of energy and enthusiasm, you'll come up with something that's exciting to other people as well. And what's more, you'll probably come up with a concept that's cohesive.

Basically, that's what I did. I decided there was room in Madison for a store with gourmet-quality coffees and teas and good accessories and really knowledgeable salespeople. I knew customers would enjoy it because we were specialized, we could answer questions and offer some things that someone who didn't specialize in coffee and tea couldn't offer. We always had a pot on. In the beginning, you could point to any coffee or tea and we'd make you a cup. So, it was very special service.

GOLDBERG: I've heard it said that you shouldn't go into a business because of a fascination with the merchandise, whether it's clothes or coffee or baseball gear, but because there's a need in the area for that merchandise.

MONDRAY: Let me say also that you shouldn't go into a business that you don't know and don't care about. That's equally bad. I think you do need expertise in your business. Whether you take it home with you at night is something else, but if you want to be the King of Pizza, you better know pizza before you sell it.

SCHROEDER: I think that it's important to know about and make use of the resources available to you. Almost every city has access to a small business administration office and many also have a program that assigns retired small business people to act as advisers for new businesses. I know of people who have used their advisers very regularly.

I also want to mention the concept of forming an advisory committee. This isn't something I had heard of back when I went into business, but I've been asked to serve in this capacity for new businesses since then. The idea is to bring together a group of knowledgeable people from different business backgrounds, take them out to dinner or whatever, present your idea to them, and get their advice. As Victor said, most people are very willing to share what they've learned.

GOLDBERG: How was that first year for you, Victor? Were you able to make a living from your shop right away?

MONDRAY: I made as much as I needed to make, probably $6–8,000 the first year. For a lot of people that wouldn't have been enough, but since I was single and living modestly, it was plenty for me. I also got my coffee free.

GOLDBERG: How much are you making now, in the third year?

MONDRAY: I think it will be between $15–20,000 this year.

GOLDBERG: Is that a comfortable living for you?

MONDRAY: I'm still reinvesting most of it at this point. Nevertheless, as I told a friend the other day, I almost never think twice about anything under $50, so it must be comfortable enough.

GOLDBERG: Carol, from all appearances, your business is thriving.

SCHROEDER: I'm making a very comfortable living from the business, but it's taken eight years to stop reinvesting most of what we make. The thing I'm most pleased with is that not only are my husband and I making a comfortable living, but we have eighteen employees, some full-time, some part-time. In a way, I feel that it's an accomplishment on our part that we're able to provide them with jobs.

GOLDBERG: I know things haven't always felt so secure as they must now. Would you describe for us what it was like to open your business?

SCHROEDER: The first two years, my husband and I would often come home from the store as late as two in the morning. We're in an area where there were a lot of new businesses, and there would be other lights on in the stores, other people working those kinds of long hours. That's one reason I'd like to emphasize how important it is to have a spouse who is supportive. It's not necessary to be involved in the business, but the spouse needs to understand how many hours it takes.

I think it's also important to have employees from the start, so you don't do it all yourself. On the other hand, you do have to pitch in and do a little of everything, to set an example for your employees.

GOLDBERG: Were your hours that long the first year, Victor?

MONDRAY: I probably worked ten to fourteen hours, six or seven days a week, depending on the time of year. For me, working has actually been the easiest part. It was some of those early days when I just sat there all dressed up with no place to go that got me down. I'd think, "My gosh, if there was a customer here, I'd be so much happier. What can I do about that?" And the answer was probably, "Nothing, except hope and keep doing what you're doing and have faith in what you're doing."

GOLDBERG: What have been the most enjoyable parts of owning a small business for you, Carol?

SCHROEDER: I'm a people person and I enjoy working with my employees and the interaction with my customers, especially when someone comes in and says, "I just love your store." That makes my day! Of course, I love the merchandise, that helps too. I don't love all of it, but most of it.

GOLDBERG: Can you describe a typical day in your business?

SCHROEDER: I do a lot of buying and spend much of my time meeting with representatives from different companies. We buy from about 500 different suppliers, and my husband and I buy for different areas of the store.

I'm also in charge of the staff, and coaching and counseling, as it's called, takes a lot of my time. Being an employer is something that many people don't have any training or experience in—it's often learned on the job. In fact, occasionally people go into business for themselves *because* they couldn't stand their last employer. Suddenly they're the one in charge and they have to develop a management style.

Beyond that, I wait on customers, plan advertising campaigns, and deal with little nitty-gritty programs like running out of toilet paper. When you're the boss, the responsibility for all those things is ultimately yours.

GOLDBERG: Victor, is your part in the day-to-day operation of your store this varied?

MONDRAY: About two years ago I started roasting my own coffee and importing my own tea. Since then, I've become a manufacturer in a sense, and my own role has become very specialized. About two-thirds of my own time is spent with coffee and tea and one-third with business. While I'm working with the coffee I'm always looking at the business, but the coffee work is so specialized that if I didn't devote a lot of time to it, I couldn't have the quality control that's necessary. I have employees who do much of the buying and help with the business.

GOLDBERG: As far as your education is concerned, are you glad you went the route of getting the degrees you did, rather than getting business degrees?

SCHROEDER: Definitely. I've found that having a liberal arts background is very enriching in my personal life. One of the concerns I have about the future of my business is personal burn-out. I've known shop owners who've lost interest in their business after twenty or twenty-five years. There are no new challenges for them.

In my case, in addition to running my shop, I write and I do translations from Danish to English. If my business isn't very rewarding for a time, if it loses its challenge at some point, there are other things that help keep life interesting for me.

GOLDBERG: Am I hearing that this business is a living, but that your basic interests are elsewhere?

SCHROEDER: No. What I'm saying is it isn't my *only* interest. Certainly it takes up a larger portion of my time than anything I do with Danish, but I'm glad that I have the option of doing both.

GOLDBERG: Victor, is your background in general science useful in your business?

MONDRAY: Oh, yes. The science background is good for concentration and the ability to look at numbers, feel comfortable with them, play with them. Also, I had quite a few chemistry courses and that background helps when I read technical manuals on coffee and coffee brewing.

I'm also sorry that I've forgotten so much of the French I learned in college and I wish I'd taken German and Spanish; it'd be terrific as an importer to be able to communicate better with the firms I deal with.

GOLDBERG: If you could do it all over again, would you still choose that route rather than getting a master's in business?

MONDRAY: I'd probably want to do both. I wouldn't mind having a little more business background now, but I really think that having started as an outsider I have a little more chutzpah than I would have otherwise.

GOLDBERG: Translate that word.

MONDRAY: Gumption.

GOLDBERG: What are your parting words of wisdom for people thinking of going into small business?

SCHROEDER: I would suggest that you start by getting a job in the field. I wouldn't open my own store, if I had a choice, without at least a year or two of work for someone else, to get an idea of what's involved in being a store owner. But then, when I did open my business, I wouldn't do it in competition with the person who gave me my background. I think that that's only fair to the person who's taught you what you know.

GOLDBERG: And what would you suggest for somebody who's decided to take the risk and open a small business?

MONDRAY: Don't burn your bridges. If you're a schoolteacher, open your business in the summer and see how it goes. If it goes great, give up your job. If it goes so-so, try it again next summer. If you can do it without burning your bridges, you'll sleep a lot better at night.

GOLDBERG: I've learned a great deal from both of you. Let me try to summarize some of what you've said.

It's possible to open a small business and be successful without a business background, but a course or a few courses in business-related subjects would be very helpful. Planning is essential, and it's a good idea to talk with, or better yet, work for, owners of similar businesses. Get comfortable with numbers. Project what you're going to sell, and figure out realistically what your costs will be. Write those projections down, and if they seem promising and you decide to take the plunge, realize that it's still a gamble.

CHAPTER 18

Retail Manager

It's hard to find time later in life to study French or philoso-phy or economics or statistics. But you will get a chance later in life to learn the nitty-gritty details of business, and they're not that hard to come by in retail management. Af-ter college, it's on-the-job training for the rest of one's life, all the way to chairman of the board.

—*Jon Hughes*

JON HUGHES and KATHY WINTERS might have been highly skep-tical during their college years if they'd been told that they'd pursue careers in retail management. Both expected that the jobs they took years ago helping customers on the sales floor were temporary, yet at this point, both are enthusiastic about the rewards of careers in retailing. Jon earned a bachelor's in history from Beloit College and began working at the J. C. Penney Company three and a half years ago, selling photo-graphic equipment. Kathy has a degree in elementary educa-tion from the University of South Florida and found a job ten years ago on the sales floor of Prange's, a midwestern depart-ment store chain. As further evidence of their contentment with their jobs, Kathy and Jon are still with those same compa-nies.

GOLDBERG: Jon, what's your job title at J. C. Penney?

HUGHES: I'm a merchandise manager for a department that in-cludes cards and luggage and women's accessories. I buy merchandise for that department and see to it that it gets out onto the floor and is maintained and sold properly.

GOLDBERG: And Kathy, what's your title at Prange's?

WINTERS: My title is general merchandise manager; the store is divided into six general areas, so I have six area managers who report to me.

GOLDBERG: If you and Jon worked in the same store, would you be Jon's boss?

WINTERS: Yes, I would.

GOLDBERG: And where did you begin?

WINTERS: I entered on the floor, coming in as a sales associate, and I became an area manager eighteen months later. The normal route from there is to go to our central buying office, first as an assistant buyer and then as a buyer. Then you might either go back in-store as an individual merchandise manager or stay in the central office as a manager of a certain division of merchandise.

GOLDBERG: Is the route that clearly defined at J. C. Penney, Jon?

HUGHES: It's similar. I think many people entering the company from now on will have college degrees and will probably enter in the management training program, rather than coming in on the selling floor.

GOLDBERG: How did you enter?

HUGHES: On the sales floor, three and a half years ago.

GOLDBERG: Have you moved up unusually quickly?

HUGHES: Yes, but I think it was atypical and luck had a lot to do with it: I was in the right place at the right time. I was promoted to merchandise manager trainee within six months and it really had to do with the fact that two managers were transferred to other positions, so that there were openings to fill. Otherwise, it would have been longer, a year or a year and a half.

GOLDBERG: Why did you choose that first job at Penney's?

HUGHES: I'd been in Europe and when I came back to Madison, it was the first job I got. It was a camera sales job and I'm a camera nut. I enjoyed it and the pay was adequate for the time and place and it led to better things.

GOLDBERG: So there's the possibility of marketing yourself via a special interest or field of expertise that may have nothing to do with your formal education.

HUGHES: That's true, although in retailing, once people get be-

yond the selling floor, specialized interests or skills are not as important as ability to do a broad variety of tasks.

GOLDBERG: But it's a way in the door.

HUGHES: That it is.

GOLDBERG: Kathy, how did you get started in this business?

WINTERS: I graduated in 1972 and I went to Europe. My husband was in the Navy and we were out of the country for almost a
year and a half. When we came back to Madison, I hoped to find a
job teaching elementary school, which is what my degree qualifies
me to do. But the teaching field was completely full. There was an
ad in the paper for retail sales at Prange's and I went there with the
hopes of only staying a few months until I got that teaching job. I've
been there now for ten years.

GOLDBERG: Some people with a college degree might feel that it
would be a comedown to work on a sales floor at a department
store. I'm wondering how, emotionally, one deals with that? Was it
a problem for you?

WINTERS: Not really. I moved up very quickly within the company and the money was there for me. Once I got into it, I loved it
and I wouldn't leave it now. I couldn't see myself as a teacher now.
In fact, I teach every day in my position. I have new people coming
to me continuously for training.

GOLDBERG: What did your first promotion mean?

WINTERS: It meant that I would have ten people working for me.
I would distribute all the paper work, see that all the merchandise
moved to the floor and was properly set up, and that sales were ar-
ranged. I would take care of all the advertising and the employee
schedules and I would be acting store manager one night every
other weekend.

GOLDBERG: That sounds like a big step. What came next?

WINTERS: It was more or less a lateral promotion, to another
store with a larger area of responsibility. Then I was promoted into
the department store from the budget store, with still more responsibility, more volume, a different area.

GOLDBERG: How many promotions have you had in ten years
with Prange's?

WINTERS: Probably about six. There are frequent openings in retail because there's such a high turnover.

GOLDBERG: And why the high turnover?

WINTERS: Probably the money. The only way to make more

money is to move, jump companies or go to the buying offices. And there are a lot of women in retail, a lot of married women who are going with their husband's careers.

GOLDBERG: Meaning an abundance of people willing to work for lower pay?

WINTERS: Yes.

HUGHES: I try to compare it to other professions. I definitely make more than teachers do, for the level of experience, and I think my bosses make very good money. I would guess that the salary level of the position immediately above me is about $35,000. That would be at a store in a large city with very good sales. At a store with less merchandise and fewer sales, in a smaller town, salaries would be lower, more comparable to the pay scale of the surrounding community.

GOLDBERG: I'd like to be a little clearer about how people are paid in retail management from the entry level on up through their years in the business.

WINTERS: If you enter as a sales associate, you usually make minimum wage. There are chances then for you to move into other departments to make a commission. If you are in our furniture department, for example, you could make up to $25,000 a year, just in sales, on commission. Our cosmetic area also offers a commission.

After sales, you'd become an area manager and be salaried at about $16,000 a year. If you come in as a management trainee, fresh out of college, you'll probably make about $15,000. That's a lot for a new person, but we have to be competitive.

GOLDBERG: And then, as you move up the ladder?

WINTERS: Assistant buyers make about $18–19,000 and buyers about $25,000. A divisional merchandise manager makes $25–30,000, and a store manager's range would probably be $48–65,000.

HUGHES: As a general rule in retailing, people start at around $15,000, and for every year they're being promoted and moving in the company, their salary will increase about $1,500. By the time they're forty, if they're on the fast track, if they're going places, they can expect to be making in the $50,000 range.

GOLDBERG: How about the first step, getting your foot in the door? I would assume that it's not too hard to get a job selling merchandise on the retail floor.

HUGHES: It's not hard at all. If you're a good worker, you can pretty much be assured of a full-time job.

GOLDBERG: How do you go about it?

HUGHES: I wouldn't necessarily wait for a position to be advertised in the newspaper. We have a rolling application process. When we need someone, we look in the files, cull the best, and call them in for interviews.

GOLDBERG: What will that first experience be like—the day-to-day life of someone who's selling?

WINTERS: You constantly have customers coming to you and you have to constantly approach customers, but you also have a manager who gives you paper work and stock work and you're expected to do it all at once. Ultimately, however, that customer comes first, and the management will be hounding you to approach that customer.

GOLDBERG: Jon, when you were selling, what did you like best about it, and what part of it was hardest for you?

HUGHES: I think the thing I enjoyed most about selling was dealing with the public, but dealing with the *friendly* public. You also have to deal with the unfriendly public. That's part of the job too.

I think the least enjoyable part of the work for me was the counting.

GOLDBERG: Counting?

HUGHES: Counting merchandise for inventory reports and mark-ups and so forth. I enjoyed that sort of tedious aspect less.

GOLDBERG: It sounds like what's needed for the sales floor is a person who likes to talk with people and who can put up once in a while with unpleasant customers and some tedious aspects of the job.

How long do you think it would be before a person who's selling can expect a substantial improvement in position?

WINTERS: I think if someone's energetic and a proven good worker, he or she can be recognized right off the bat within our company.

GOLDBERG: And how different from selling is that new position with supervisory and buying responsibilities?

HUGHES: My present job is very hectic and it requires a lot of juggling. I have a clipboard on which I keep track of pressing issues that need to be attended to that day, and it usually has about twelve items listed. In an eight- or nine- or ten-hour day, you don't have much time for each of those items, especially considering the fact that about half of your day will be taken up with filler, little things that can't be anticipated.

GOLDBERG: What are the categories of those items?

HUGHES: I guess the most time-comsuming would be merchandising: checking up on orders or writing the orders. That probably constitutes 40 percent of my time.

GOLDBERG: Do you make decisions about what merchandise to buy? For instance, could you pick out a kind of luggage for Penney's to carry, even if they've never carried it before.

HUGHES: If it's offered through an authorized price list that Penney's puts out, yes. It would be like going to the Penney's catalog. That's what I can buy.

GOLDBERG: That sounds like fun.

HUGHES: It can be, yes. We have some merchandisers who are real artists, who bring in what we call "forward-looking" merchandise. They're successful and enjoy their work, but they're under the same pressure I am. They have to deal with the hectic pace and realize that you cannot be a perfectionist, you've got to do the task at hand and not look back.

GOLDBERG: It sounds like you're a little overworked.

HUGHES: I would say so, yes.

GOLDBERG: You say 40 percent of your time is spent buying and selecting merchandise. How do you spend the other 60 percent?

HUGHES: I'd say another 30 percent might be personnel: communications, meetings, and so on.

GOLDBERG: How many people are in your department?

HUGHES: Right now, which is a low time, I'm supervising about twenty people. At the peak it's close to fifty.

GOLDBERG: That's a lot of folks. And the other 30 percent of your time?

HUGHES: I spend a lot of time tallying up my sales results. Knowing where your sales are at any one time is very valued in the organization, and the people who do are targeted as being on the fast track.

GOLDBERG: Is there a lot of competition in that fast track?

HUGHES: No, other than friendly competition among the merchandisers. I think the emphasis at Penney's is to have the merchandisers be as much of a team as possible. The merchandise lines do overlap and the areas overlap, and therefore cooperation helps the total store.

GOLDBERG: When you're an area manager, is it like running your own store?

HUGHES: My boss makes a point of saying, "If this were your own store, what would you do?"

GOLDBERG: Kathy, do you tell the six area managers you supervise that they're each running a store?

WINTERS: Yes, I do. They're running their own departments and they don't compete with each other. They help each other.

In our company, the job descriptions of the area managers are changing right now. We're going to what's called "job by function," which means that rather than trying to do all things within an area, the managers' role will be specialized. They'll be merchandisers, job analysts, or controllers for the entire store. This change means they'll be communicating with each other daily. They won't be able to work independently of each other anymore, as they do now.

GOLDBERG: How frequently do liberal arts grads come into the management training programs now?

WINTERS: We hire trainees every six months. Representatives from the company go to campuses and recruit, and people also apply to enter the training program. A lot of the trainees are business majors, but certainly not all of them. We've had just about every kind of major.

If you become a trainee, you'll start right on the selling floor. We believe that you have to learn sales first of all, and there's usually a six- to eight-month wait before the first promotion.

GOLDBERG: So in essence, it's the same as just coming in with a job on the sales floor, except I bet the pay is higher as a trainee.

WINTERS: Yes. If you start out as a management trainee, you'll be salaried.

GOLDBERG: Then, if you want to go into retailing, and you're not accepted in a management training program, you don't have to wait. You can start by selling on the retail floor, proving yourself there.

WINTERS: That's right.

GOLDBERG: You said, Jon, that perhaps the worst part of your present job is that there's too much to do and too little time. Any other difficult parts?

HUGHES: That really hits the nail on the head. It's a very demanding job. You can work long hours and you will just never get done. I think you've got to look at a fifty-hour week as your norm.

GOLDBERG: Does this kind of career affect your home life?

HUGHES: Yes, but probably not to the same degree as a profession like law or medicine.

GOLDBERG: How about for you, Kathy? Is your workweek fifty hours or more or less?

WINTERS: Forty-eight to fifty hours every week. I have one child, and it's a problem at home sometimes. My husband works better hours. He's off earlier in the day, so we work it out.

GOLDBERG: Do you work evenings, weekends?

WINTERS: Yes. Everything is planned around my schedule, always. Within the family, we always check with my schedule first.

HUGHES: We have a rotating system for evenings and weekends. I work one night a week and one out of four weekends, which I don't begrudge that much. In fact, it offers a change of pace. I also have occasional three-day weekends, and I can sometimes come in late in the morning, so it's a varied schedule.

GOLDBERG: Kathy, do you have such a good schedule?

WINTERS: Not quite. We rotate every other weekend and we work one fifteen-hour day every week, coming in at eight o'clock and staying until closing.

GOLDBERG: You both have liberal arts degrees. Now that you're in retailing, are you glad that you got those degrees?

HUGHES: Very definitely. I don't see the need for a specialized marketing or business degree for my position or probably 75 or 80 percent of the jobs at the Penney Company.

It's hard to find time later in life to study French or philosophy or economics or statistics. But you will get a chance later in life to learn the nitty-gritty details of business, and they're not that hard to come by in retail management. After college, it's on-the-job training for the rest of one's life, all the way to chairman of the board.

GOLDBERG: Is there anything you got out of your liberal arts education that's useful in your job?

HUGHES: I think the seminar approach that Beloit College offers was very good training. Working in small groups, learning to speak clearly and to fine-tune your ideas and your presentation can be very valuable. You also learn that other people can shed light on your own thinking, and that's important to know in any work situation.

GOLDBERG: Kathy, do you wish you'd gotten a business degree?

WINTERS: No. I'm glad I have a teaching degree. Most of my job involves training and teaching.

GOLDBERG: Do you like the people in retailing, the people you work with?

WINTERS: I do. I like all the people that I work with at this point. We've been selective and we've gotten people who like other people. We're a good group.

GOLDBERG: In every field there are stereotypes, and usually they're not justified, but do you think there's such a thing as a typical retail manager?

WINTERS: No, I don't think so. I would say, though, that a retailer has to like people and have a high energy and stamina level.

GOLDBERG: Do you buy that, Jon?

HUGHES: Yes. A retailer needs to be personable and have high standards. And I think the combination of those two qualities is almost unstoppable. If you're pleasant, hardworking, and intelligent, the career is out there in retail.

What did surprise me was that the business world is not as cold as I had thought it might be from my perspective as a liberal arts graduate. I really like the camaraderie that exists in retail.

GOLDBERG: Jon, where do you hope to be in your career in five years?

HUGHES: I think I could expect to be at Kathy's level.

GOLDBERG: And Kathy?

WINTERS: I'd like to be a store manager. And I think that will happen in fewer than five years.

GOLDBERG: Do you have any tips for people who might want to go into retailing?

WINTERS: You have to be a good communicator and have good writing skills, and some experience in merchandising certainly helps.

HUGHES: It's very important to take elementary math courses. I'm not talking about algebra or calculus, but you're going to be working with percentages and rate of sales and trends and such, and you do need to be very comfortable doing that.

GOLDBERG: In the future, do you think that careers in retailing will remain abundant?

WINTERS: There's always an opening in retail.

GOLDBERG: In summary, one of the most important and interesting things I've learned is that retail management is a very accessible career. Openings on the sales floor are easy to find, and once you're selling, your potential for moving up is great. There's a lot of variety in the steps up the retail ladder, from selling to supervising to buying, and eventually, to running the whole store. For a person with an outgoing personality, a tolerance for a certain amount or routine and tedious work, and a good measure of flexibility, a career in retail management might be well worth considering.

CHAPTER 19

TV and Radio Producer

People become producers for public TV because they love it. Generally, they'll grouse about their low pay, but then they stop and think about it and they say, "Yeah, but I get to do my thing." There's a tremendous amount of freedom associated with the job.

—Dan Peterson

DAN PETERSON, ALICIA ALLEN, and VICKI NONN are media producers. Dan works for a public television station where, after years of program production, he has recently become an executive producer. Alicia produces local news shows for an NBC affiliate, and Vicki works for Wisconsin Public Radio, where she produces primarily cultural programs. As they point out, though television and radio production may conjure visions of glamor, excitement, fast pace, and high pay, the greater part of the reality is solid hard work. Regardless, judging from the stiff competition for entry-level jobs, the appeal of a media career is enormous.

GOLDBERG: Dan, you got your bachelor's degree in—

PETERSON: English literature with a minor in French literature. I've also done some graduate work in medieval literature and several dead languages: Old Norse, Old Icelandic, and Old English.

GOLDBERG: Alicia, how about you?

ALLEN: I got a bachelor's in political science, with all intentions of going to law school.

GOLDBERG: And Vicki?

NONN: I have a bachelor's degree in music education and a master's degree in organ.

GOLDBERG: Typical backgrounds for media producers! We have here three people who are all successful in television or radio production, none of whom have degrees in communication arts or broadcasting.

What is a producer, Alicia?

ALLEN: Something like a traffic cop. A producer has to keep track of where everybody's going and make sure they're all going in the right direction at the right time and that they all end up at the right place. The producer has to make decisions about which stories are going to be shot, where they're going to be shot, who's going to do them, how long they'll run, etc. And in news, which is what I produce, all that can change from moment to moment.

GOLDBERG: As I understand it, you produce two news shows.

ALLEN: Actually, I'm doing three now. I do the five and the six o'clock news with another producer and the ten o'clock by myself.

GOLDBERG: Vicki, is being a producer for public radio that varied?

NONN: A producer has a lot of different functions in radio, too. Sometimes we're involved in creative work and sometimes in administrative details, filling in the blanks.

GOLDBERG: Which do you do more of?

NONN: I guess I'd have to say filling in the blanks.

PETERSON: I think the traffic cop analogy is largely accurate wherever you're producing, but one thing you have less of in public broadcasting than in commercial is focus. In public TV, we produce everything from soup to nuts. This means a producer works with many different clients on many different types of projects, all of which have different applications, different markets, and different audiences.

I think the primary criterion for being a public TV producer, at least in a shop like ours, is that you be a generalist and an information omnivor. You have to have a lust for learning things and you have to be able to put yourself in the position of someone in the audience who doesn't know very much about your subject.

GOLDBERG: Alicia, how did you become involved in television?

ALLEN: For about four and a half years, I worked in public relations for the city of Baltimore, and I think what roped me into television was working on projects for the city that involved radio and

TV. I had media people as my contacts and I got to know more and more about their business.

As for actual television work, I have to admit that I literally stumbled through the door. I came to Madison to go to graduate school and during my second year, I heard someone mention a minority internship with the local NBC affiliate. I thought, "Why not give it a shot?" And it worked. I had no intention of doing that at the time, but the opportunity presented itself and I was lucky.

GOLDBERG: What did you do during the internship?

ALLEN: Any number of things. I started in film, splicing together a daily spot reel of commercials and making sure they ran in the right places in movies. And of course, they started me with the worst shift possible, with just weekends and nights. After a few months, I moved into production: running cameras, doing lighting, learning about sound. And eventually, I worked in news.

GOLDBERG: Do internships pay enough to live on?

ALLEN: Of course not.

GOLDBERG: Were you working full-time?

ALLEN: No. I worked sixteen hours a week and then twenty, and after about a year, twenty-five or thirty. The kind of person who pursues a TV career only does it because they love the business, not because they want to get rich. And you either love it or you hate it.

GOLDBERG: Dan, what can you tell us about breaking into public TV?

PETERSON: Like any other discipline or profession, there are ways to get your foot in the door. The question is, do you really want to be there?

Broadcasting is a notoriously poor profession in terms of pay scale. Most people are attracted to it because they want to be producers. Very few people, especially young people, can see themselves as administrators, but that's where the money is in broadcasting. Production is a dead end in terms of money and professional advancement. If you're planning a long career in broadcasting, you'd better be certain that it's what you want to do, because the major reward is getting the job done and believe me, getting the job done is filled with one headache after another.

ALLEN: In my work, too, getting the job done day to day is a grind. It's not a glamorous profession, but still, there's just something about the people in the business that I like a lot. And when you come into the station, you're charged up because you don't know what's going to come at you. That's one of the attractions the job holds for me.

I think in some way people believe television is magical and the people who produce it have an incredible amount of power. And they may have, in terms of shaping attitudes and ideas. But it can be a heavy burden when you realize that decisions you make about how a story looks or sounds may shape someone's life.

NONN: I think radio is less powerful, especially public radio, in shaping what people do with their lives. My own productions tend to be more culturally oriented.

GOLDBERG: For example?

NONN: Right now I'm working on a live chamber concert series, and a series of programs of folk music recordings made back in the forties.

GOLDBERG: Do you think that kind of production is as pressured as television?

NONN: There's a lot of pressure in my job. There's a lot of juggling several things at once, switching gears, not being able to concentrate on a project when you need to.

GOLDBERG: Vicki, how did you get into this business?

NONN: As a typist.

GOLDBERG: And how did you move from there?

NONN: There was an opening and I applied for the position and was accepted. Then my boss offered to let me do a little production, a very small instructional music program. I liked that and gradually I did more and more production. This place is great at providing opportunities to explore new aspects of the radio business.

GOLDBERG: What does a radio producer do all day? What's a day in your life like?

NONN: There really isn't a typical day. I do some script writing, I time things, I edit tape, I mix the elements, the music and the talk. If I'm producing a live show, then I have to coordinate with performers and engineers. And while we're taping, I direct from the control room.

GOLDBERG: What's that like?

NONN: You nudge people in the direction you'd like to have them go in. They have a script already and they'll be reading it or they might be ad-libbing. And you listen and critique.

GOLDBERG: Is it very hard to break into broadcasting?

ALLEN: Yes, because there are a lot of very talented people out there who want in. And I think the ones who make it are the ones who are most aggressive and stick with it, who are at your door with ideas, selling themselves and saying, "This is what makes me different, makes me special."

GOLDBERG: How did you break in, Dan?

PETERSON: I was in graduate school and had no particular interest in television. I was working on a local theatrical production with a friend and he asked if I'd help him with a little free-lance job he had at a public television station, writing music for an instructional TV series. So we did that and got invited back to do more music for them, and eventually, they offered me a job writing twenty-six original half-hour programs. And fool that I was, I said, "I can do that."

About three months into the project, the producer was in an accident and they simply threw equipment at the rest of us and said, "Go produce it." And we did. And everything I've learned about production, from that point on, has been simply by going out and doing it.

GOLDBERG: Alicia, describe your typical workday for us.

ALLEN: I start work at two o'clock, so the first thing I want to know when I get to the station is what's been shot in the morning hours. I want to have a list of stories and what they're about and some general idea about where they'll run in the newscast. If we've got any live shots, I want to know where and who's doing them. I might make some phone calls and in general catch up with what's happened since I listened to the morning news on the radio or read a morning newspaper.

Of course some days the place is in an uproar. Something has happened and if I walk into the middle of it, I don't have time to sit around and recap the day. It means I jump in and do whatever needs to be done at the time.

GOLDBERG: Can you give us an idea about how much of your time is spent doing which chores?

ALLEN: I'd say 80 percent of my day is spent making sure that people have what they need. I do a lot of running, not in errand types of thing, but just being where people need me to be. Someone might need to have their copy checked, someone might have a broken camera, someone might be lost or running late, that kind of thing.

GOLDBERG: So, you're a planner, a go-for, a secretary, and a producer in the classical sense of making decisions. You're wearing twenty hats a day. Aren't you going to burn out?

ALLEN: I doubt it.

GOLDBERG: But how does anyone survive that kind of pressure?

ALLEN: I work out every day. I get it out in the gym. I learned the hard way that I need to physically remove myself from that newsroom some time during the day and take the time to do something for myself.

GOLDBERG: Dan, are the pressures of public television similar?

PETERSON: Yes. Perhaps even greater because we're doing so many more different kinds of projects. And I think Alicia is right on the button: your final job as a producer is to take care of yourself. If you can't keep yourself fresh, you're not going to do anything for anybody else.

GOLDBERG: I know that you're an executive producer now and that much of your time is spent with administrative work. But back when you were only producing programs, how was your time spent?

PETERSON: About 80 percent of it was spent running, jumping through hoops, checking things out, taking care of other people.

If you're a producer, you have to have tremendous confidence that you're going to be able to pull it off, that you're not going to fail. You can't question that, but on the other hand, you have to have the ability to work with other people, and in some ways, those qualities are contradictory.

GOLDBERG: Is a producer partly an artist?

PETERSON: Yes, and partly bookkeeper, den mother, and therapist.

GOLDBERG: Let me ask you all this: if you were hiring assistants, what would determine who you'd hire?

ALLEN: I'd hire someone who has good writing and organizational skills and who isn't going to fall apart when things don't go according to plan. I think what makes or breaks producers is whether they're adaptable, whether they can handle hour by hour what's being thrown at them.

PETERSON: Walter Cronkite said in an interview several years ago that he'd never hire anybody for television production who didn't have at least five years of experience writing for a good newspaper. I think that if somebody were to come to me with those credentials, I'd hire them on the spot.

At an entry-level position, I would put a great deal of emphasis on the ability to write, to think, and to ask questions. Producers can't be people who are looking for answers; they need to be people who can ask the next question.

NONN: The most important thing for me is that it be someone I can work with well, whose personality meshes with mine. They also need to be flexible, and to have a little mechanical aptitude. They don't have to be able to cut tape, but they can't be all thumbs either.

GOLDBERG: Are there special qualities that are needed for radio as opposed to television?

NONN: I'd look for people who use their ears a lot, who have been trained to listen carefully and to notice things.

GOLDBERG: And if someone had a degree in communication arts or broadcasting, would that impress you?

NONN: No. I think I'd be careful of that person.

ALLEN: I would too.

GOLDBERG: Why?

ALLEN: Because I think sometimes those people have preconceived notions about what they're supposed to do in the business, and they shut out all other avenues. And often, broadcasting students are turned out the same way, writing in the same style, without many fresh ideas. It's nice to have people come in from different fields. They bring a new dimension to the business, and that makes it exciting.

GOLDBERG: Before we move on, what are we leaving out in terms of ways to break into media production?

PETERSON: One important way is to volunteer your services. You can simply jump in, help out, be around, make yourself visible. It's a way of making sure a career in broadcasting is what you want, and when an opportunity comes, you'll be in a good position to know about it and to present yourself well. I've seen a lot of people get into this business simply because they were there at the right time and they were smart enough to get involved.

GOLDBERG: Alicia, what if a person walked into your station and volunteered to do some work for free, just for the sake of being around and learning something about the business?

ALLEN: I think that kind of offer would take everybody by surprise, but I'd love to use a person who doesn't know what to expect or have preconceived notions about the job.

GOLDBERG: I heard on National Public Radio that the lowest-paid professionals in the country right now are journalists in public radio, followed by public TV, followed by teaching. Does that sound accurate?

NONN: Probably.

GOLDBERG: After years of being a producer, what can someone expect to make in public radio?

NONN: I'd say $20,000.

GOLDBERG: Dan, how about in public television? Where can you go if you don't move to management, if you stay in production?

PETERSON: In terms of salary, not very far. I think that you're always going to be making less than a public school teacher. And one reason is that everybody wants your job, so you have no leverage.

People become producers for public TV because they love it. Generally, they'll grouse about their low pay, but then they stop and think about it and they say, "Yeah, but I get to do my thing." There's a tremendous amount of freedom associated with the job.

GOLDBERG: Alicia, I would guess a producer working for commercial television would be better paid.

ALLEN: Not really. I'm not making a heck of a lot more now than I was before I came to graduate school.

GOLDBERG: What about all these big-shot TV producers at the major networks?

PETERSON: It's the tip of the iceberg. Ninety-five or 99 percent of the people who work as producers work in small markets, where the only people who are making money are the station manager and the administrators and the station owners.

ALLEN: And realistically, you learn more in the smaller markets and the lower-paying jobs.

GOLDBERG: What advice on skills and courses would you offer people who would like to break into broadcasting?

ALLEN: Lately, I've been mentioning to people that a good computer course would be helpful. And they should hone their writing skills. One of my pet peeves is graduates who can't write precise, simple, direct sentences.

GOLDBERG: Even liberal arts graduates?

PETERSON: Especially liberal arts graduates. It's deplorable.

Another fundamental and necessary talent for a producer is the ability to tell a story clearly, concisely, and in a compelling way. Whether you're producing cultural programs for public broadcasting or news for a commercial affiliate, you have to remember that television is a medium that first, last, and always communicates through the emotions. Any information that you're going to relay moves through the gut.

Radio is very different. I know Vicki can verify that it's a much more flexible medium in terms of ideas and being able to explore things in depth. Television is like the Platte River. It's a mile wide and an inch deep and you just have to live with that.

GOLDBERG: Vicki, if someone offered you a job producing for television, what would you say?

NONN: No, thanks.

GOLDBERG: Why?

NONN: I like radio and I like the possibilities that it offers. I might try television, but I think I'd come back to radio. For one thing, it's what I'm used to, but also, there are so many possibilities that I still want to explore.

GOLDBERG: In summary, it's very tough to get your foot in the door in radio and television, and you may have to start as a volunteer or a typist or an intern. If you find a job as an assistant producer, you can consider yourself very lucky. Once there, the pay is lousy, the glamor is fleeting, the work is hard, and the pressure can be severe. Despite all of this, lots and lots of people want to produce for TV and radio. Why? Probably in great measure due to the freedom and creativity that come with the territory.

CHAPTER 20

Real Estate Agent

.

The thing I value most about real estate, and one of the main reasons I'm still in it, is the independence that it offers. I have the freedom to come and go and I don't have to report to anybody or account for my activities—unless, of course, I'm not producing.

—Libby Monson

LIBBY MONSON and ANDY SYMANSKI are old hands in the home real estate business. Andy became a realtor fifteen years ago, after a six-year career as a professional soldier. Recently, he's undertaken a management position while continuing to sell homes. Libby has been a realtor for eleven years, after an initial career as a parole officer with the Department of Corrections and several years of homemaking. One of the points Libby and Andy emphasize is how very much the real estate business has changed since their early days selling homes. Another major point: the fair-weather nature of the business.

GOLDBERG: Libby, in your experience, is there such a things as a typical day in real estate?

MONSON: On a typical day, I spend more time in the office than out of it, even though the goal is to be out working with a prospect or showing a house. I've been meaning to count how many phone calls I make or receive in any given day—I'd say that often it's about twenty or twenty-five. I talk to my sellers, meaning people whose homes I've listed, and to potential sellers and buyers. I talk to loan officers, to other realtors, and to other real estate companies. And always, the ultimate goal is to list and sell homes, to make a commission.

GOLDBERG: Let's clarify what you do and how you make money. First, you get a contract from a seller to list his or her property for a period of time. That's called a listing. If you sell the property, you get a commission, which is probably anywhere from 4 to 9 percent of the sale price, depending on what you've negotiated with the seller. If someone else sells the property during the period of your listing contract, you still make a small percentage as the listing agent. If the property doesn't sell at all during the term of your contract, how much do you make for all your work?

MONSON: Zero.

GOLDBERG: What you've described so far—so many phone calls and looking for buyers and sellers—sounds a little tedious.

MONSON: It can be very tedious. I much prefer the time when I'm out there with the customer. That's the best part of it: actually working with buyers and sellers, getting to know them, being a good listener, trying to ferret out what they're really saying, what they really want. The better I understand what they're looking for, the sooner I can find that property and make the sale.

GOLDBERG: How do you find your clients?

MONSON: Sometimes I contact people who I know are planning to move. Sometimes, I receive a call from a couple who would like me to come out and see their home and tell them what it's worth. Yesterday, in the middle of a very busy day with several appointments already scheduled, I got a call from a young woman. She wanted to know more about some condominiums, and since she had the afternoon off, she wanted to know if I could take her out to see them. So, yes, I was able to fit it in and I was glad to do that because, after all, that's what it's all about.

But the day is often hard to predict. We don't know when we wake up in the morning what it will hold, except that if business is good and the prospects are there, the hours will probably be very long. My workday usually begins around nine in the morning and doesn't end before seven or eight at night. Often it goes to eleven or midnight.

GOLDBERG: When people talk about such long workdays, I'm always skeptical, because I think they may be remembering one day in the last month. Are there really a lot of days when you work that long?

MONSON: If the business is there, yes. There are many realtors who don't, but I think if you want to be successful, you have to go with the flow. You have to be available when the customers are there. And people are like bananas: they come in bunches.

GOLDBERG: Andy, do you think, based on your fifteen years of experience, that real estate is a nine-to-five profession?

SYMANSKI: No. There are three basic things that you have to do as a realtor and each one is time-consuming. You have to expose yourself to people, you have to list properties for sale, and you have to sell them. You may do one more than the other on any given day, but basically you organize your time along those lines.

GOLDBERG: Which of those three things do you spend most of your time doing?

SYMANSKI: I spend most of my time listing homes for sale. Many new salespeople try to go the other route and sell more than they list.

GOLDBERG: How can you sell a property that you haven't listed?

SYMANSKI: You can sell a property listed by an agent from another firm, but then you have to share the commission with the listing agent, so you get half the reward for the effort. Some firms also have what they call "opportunity time" or "floor time." For those given periods, any realtor can receive calls coming to their particular firm. In that way, they come in contact with people who wish to purchase properties, who are calling about a property that's being advertised by the firm.

GOLDBERG: That sounds like an easy job. You sit there and answer the phone. If someone wants to see a house, you go show it to them and you sell it.

SYMANSKI: It does sounds easy, but it's not. Most people who call about a specific advertised property don't buy that particular property. So that call simply provides the salesperson with a prospective buyer contact, but that's all it does. It doesn't sell the property for you.

Early in their careers, many realtors do concentrate on selling more than listing, because it provides income more rapidly. However, for long-term career success, it's preferable to have a balance, and if there isn't a balance I would rather have the weight swing toward listing.

GOLDBERG: I can't help but wonder if it's a little humiliating to try to get strangers to list their homes with you? Libby, is that tough?

MONSON: Yes. I remember how I started. I had just moved to this community, so I didn't know anybody, and the way I started was probably the toughest way possible: I literally went out and knocked on doors.

I would introduce myself, explain that I was in the real estate business, and ask if they knew anybody who wanted to sell or buy a home. I also called on people who were trying to sell their homes themselves. But a stranger, knocking on doors: you know how well that's received. I kept track at one point of how many owner-sellers I called on before I landed a listing: twenty-six.

GOLDBERG: Twenty-six rejections and then you got a listing?

MONSON: Yes.

GOLDBERG: How did your ego stand that?

MONSON: It was hard. I really didn't know what I was doing.

SYMANSKI: I think the problem was what you just said: a lack of training. *How* you go about knocking on that door is critical. From what you said, I'd have to make the assumption that there was no advance preparation with the homeowners. And there's no question that a cold knock on the door with no prior communication, no paving of the way, is extremely difficult. With preparation, it's not that difficult. And the rejection rate is not as high.

GOLDBERG: But in general, Andy, does a realtor have to confront rejection and learn to take it?

SYMANSKI: Yes. In fact, I'd add a fourth item to my list of a realtor's necessary skills: the ability to successfully ward off the psychological assaults of the customers.

GOLDBERG: To be able to accept rejection.

SYMANSKI: That's right. That's the name of the game: accepting rejection. But it doesn't happen as often as one might think in this business if there's adequate preparation.

GOLDBERG: That leads me to wonder about the kind of person who is successful as a realtor. How about you, Andy? Do you fit the personality profile of a successful realtor?

SYMANSKI: Yes.

GOLDBERG: Why?

SYMANSKI: To succeed in this business, you have to be tough, resilient, disciplined, and hardworking. And you have to understand—for lack of a better term—the human heart. Within each of us, there's a reasonable facsimile of every other human being, and to understand the human heart, you just have to try to place yourself in someone's elses shoes.

GOLDBERG: Libby, are you tough?

MONSON: You bet. I wouldn't have survived eleven years as a realtor if I weren't. There's another quality a realtor must have that Andy didn't mention: a high degree of self-confidence. You do have to eat a lot of rejection and if you take to heart what those people are saying, you're not going to be around very long.

GOLDBERG: I can tell by talking with you, Libby, that you have the kind of personality people warm up to. You've been in real estate for eleven years and I'm wondering whether by now your business is self-sustaining, so that you can just walk in and go to work and not have to hunt for clients or face rejection anymore?

MONSON: No. I wish that were true. Over the years, of course, I've built up a reasonably good reputation. If you stick it out in real estate and work hard, you're rewarded by having a good referral base. People give my name to their friends and relatives, so I do have people calling me. That helps.

SYMANSKI: There's quite a change after you've been in the business a few years. Early in your career, you concentrate heavily on not making mistakes. And later, with your reputation established, you do receive referrals and at that point, you're able to concentrate on getting the job done.

GOLDBERG: What kind of mistakes do you mean?

SYMANSKI: Filling out the forms correctly, having the right information, saying the right thing. All those purely mechanical parts of this business are constantly in the mind of a new salesperson.

GOLDBERG: Is it difficult to learn about those mechanics?

MONSON: Not really, but when Andy and I started in the business there weren't good training programs like there are now. Anybody who's considering going into real estate ought to understand that there are excellent training programs available. Many are provided by companies for their new employees, but there are also taped courses. Andy and I learned on the street, so to speak. We just went out there and learned by trial and error.

SYMANSKI: Local boards of realtors and national and state realty associations also provide tremendously effective training programs. Take advantage of them. Don't go through what we went through.

MONSON: There's something else that I think anyone considering this career should understand: it takes a tremendous amount of physical energy to be successful in real estate. It's not a career for somebody who wants to work a nine-to-five day and have a coffee break in the morning and a coffee break in the afternoon. You have to be flexible, you have to have a lot of energy, and you have to be able to work a twelve-, thirteen-, fourteen-hour day—and maybe three or four of them in a row.

GOLDBERG: When you work that hard, do you basically feel like you're still a salesperson or do you feel deep down like you're offering a professional service like a doctor or a lawyer?

SYMANSKI: I feel like a professional.

MONSON: Me too.

GOLDBERG: But when I hear that you have to keep prospecting even after so many successful years, I wonder how you keep up your morale. I think I'd feel like, "Here I am, trying to sell myself once more."

SYMANSKI: I think you may have misinterpreted something Libby said. We continue to prospect, but it's more a social thing at this point.

GOLDBERG: So it does get more sophisticated?

MONSON: I don't go knocking door-to-door anymore, no.

GOLDBERG: Who should go into this business and who should stay out of it?

MONSON: If someone's interested in security, no. If you want to know that there's a pay check coming every week or two, if you want to know that at the end of the year, you're going to have made X number of dollars, no. If you're not willing to work hard or if you're not comfortable taking risks, then no, you should not go into this business.

GOLDBERG: How about family? You're describing a job that's not very structured in terms of schedule, that includes work at night and on weekends. How does that affect your family life?

SYMANSKI: It does affect the family, and you have to develop an approach that will keep that to a minimum. Every day you make appointments with clients. There's no reason why you shouldn't make appointments with your family and treat them with equal seriousness. That means if you get a call from somebody who wishes to see a home right away, you tell them that you have a conflicting appointment and you'll have to show the property another time.

GOLDBERG: Is it that simple for you, Libby?

MONSON: Yes. If you don't make appointments for your social life and for your family, you'll find that you won't have time for them. So you work one night and maybe the next morning you can spend some time with your family.

The thing I value most about real estate, and one of the main reasons I'm still in it, is the independence that it offers. I have the freedom to come and go and I don't have to report to anybody or account for my activities—unless, of course, I'm not producing.

GOLDBERG: In your best year of the eleven years you've been in the business, how much did you make?

MONSON: Fifty thousand.

GOLDBERG: Your worst?

MONSON: I have to think way back to the first year. I think it was $12,900.

GOLDBERG: So you even made a living your first year. Andy?

SYMANSKI: The first year I earned $8,500. And my best year when I was just selling, before I became a manager, was about $70,000.

GOLDBERG: What do you think the average home-selling realtor makes?

MONSON: It's very low. In fact, the average realtor has only four transactions a year. That's a national statistic.

GOLDBERG: Are those full-time realtors?

MONSON: No. There are a lot of part-time realtors and I'm sure they're included in that figure.

SYMANSKI: In the area that I'm familiar with, I'd say the average income for a full-time salesperson is in the range of $18–20,000 a year.

GOLDBERG: What about the realtors you've known who have said, "I quit. I've had it." Can you describe for us why they quit?

MONSON: I think they just get really discouraged. It's hard not to when the economy goes down, when there are people who want to buy real estate, but can't because it's a financial impossibility. Those are really tough times and that's why a lot of them quit. Others do it because they want a different challenge. That's a more positive reason.

GOLDBERG: But even in those tough times, some people quit and some people stick it out like you did. So who are those people who are quitting?

SYMANSKI: Salespeople depend on just one thing and that's selling enough to live on. If they're not earning a personal income of X amount of dollars, they'll have to quit, unless they're independently wealthy.

As for why they're not doing well financially, go back to the general criteria. Although I don't believe that there's a prototype of a successful realtor, there are certain earmarks that stand one in good stead for being successful. The toughness, the resilience.

MONSON: And don't forget that there are people who stay in this business who don't do as well as those who quit.

GOLDBERG: Why would they quit if they're doing well?

MONSON: They don't like it anymore. They don't like the weekends, they don't like the nights, they don't like the uncertainty, the questions: "When am I going to get paid? What's going to happen next? Are we going to have another recession?" They want a different life-style.

GOLDBERG: After eleven years, Libby, do those things ever bother you?

MONSON: Yes, they do. But when I make money, I forget it all.

GOLDBERG: What's the biggest kick besides the check?

MONSON: Making the sale. I love it.

GOLDBERG: But that only happens for a brief moment. Does the exhilaration last?

MONSON: No, but I guess what lasts are all those people I've met. There are few opportunities to get to know people as well as you can when you're helping them buy or sell a home. There's a lot of emotional investment connected with that decision.

GOLDBERG: Andy, what are the best and the worst parts of this profession for you?

SYMANSKI: The best part is achieving the objective of the hunt: making that sale, getting that listing. And the worst part is not achieving what I've set out to achieve.

GOLDBERG: Not meeting your goals?

SYMANSKI: That's right. That gets me down.

GOLDBERG: How about your peers? Do you have any particular affinity with them: Are they a type that you'd like to be friends with any more than anybody else?

MONSON: I think so, in my company anyway. Most of the people I know well who are successful in this business are very individualistic. They're opinionated, they're forceful, dynamic, interesting, not easily pushed around.

SYMANSKI: They're fun to be around.

MONSON: You know what they think.

GOLDBERG: When I was looking for people to do this interview, I found that there are a lot of women who are successfully selling homes, but very few men. Most men in real estate are dealing in commercial property. Is residential real estate a man's field too, Andy?

SYMANSKI: Certainly.

GOLDBERG: Do you feel comfortable being a man in this business?

SYMANSKI: Very much so. I'm successful in this business.

GOLDBERG: Do you think a man has an edge in selling homes?

SYMANSKI: Yes.

MONSON: Yes, absolutely.

GOLDBERG: Why, Libby?

MONSON: Because there is a great old boy's network out there.

GOLDBERG: But you women have a semimonopoly on home sales.

MONSON: That's not really true. Nationally, it's about fifty-fifty. In our community, I'm sure there are fewer males, but if you look at who's making money selling residential real estate, it's the men.

GOLDBERG: Is it possible that that's because men have been traditionally brought up to be more assertive, to take more risks?

MONSON: Sure. But the male network is important, too. The accountant or the attorney who refers a client to a realtor is more apt to refer that client to a man.

GOLDBERG: What's the future of your field, of selling homes for a living?

SYMANSKI: I think there will be a diminishing number of realtors in home sales in the future, and not because there aren't people who wish to go into real estate. I think it's simply going to become more difficult to purchase homes.

GOLDBERG: So tight financing and high-cost mortgages are going to cut down on the sales of homes and therefore there will be fewer dollars to go around.

SYMANSKI: That's right.

MONSON: I agree. It's going to be harder and harder to make a living selling homes in the future.

GOLDBERG: In other words, it's harder to make it now than it was in the past?

MONSON: Very much so.

GOLDBERG: Is there still an influx of people coming into real estate, even though there's no bigger pie to share?

SYMANSKI: There still is an influx, but it's not as great as it was in the seventies.

MONSON: The turnover rate is tremendous, though. There are a lot of people leaving, too.

GOLDBERG: Libby, if you were a homemaker returning to the work force right now, knowing what you know about selling homes, is it the career you'd choose for a living?

MONSON: Considering my talents and abilities and my educational background, yes.

GOLDBERG: Your educational background?

MONSON: I don't type. What else can a person do?

SYMANSKI: I would do the same thing. I'd choose to come into real estate and into residential sales.

GOLDBERG: Let me summarize some of what you've said: real estate is not for the faint of heart. The successful realtor must have a high level of self-confidence, perseverance, and energy, and he or she must be able to take a lot of rejection. The hours in this business are long and time with family and friends will become precious. The major rewards of real estate are probably the freedom it offers, the nice yearly income for the very determined and skilled realtor, and the chance to know and help people in the process of buying or selling a home.

CHAPTER 21

Now What?

As I said in the Introduction, the ball is in your court. You probably don't need more than the liberal arts degree you have in hand. Within you lie the education, the abilities, and the will to obtain a joyful and meaningful career.

But what if none of these fourteen careers grabs you? It may well be that none of them is just right for you. Well, there are hundreds of careers you can obtain with a liberal arts degree. This book and its fourteen careers are meant as a guide, as a method, to show you how to do it. In my opinion, the very toughest part of the search for a career isn't the job interview, it isn't finding the hidden jobs, and it has nothing to do with writing your resume. The toughest part revolves around the key question in all important decisions in your life: *What do I want?*

I recently interviewed a woman on my radio program who is a rising star in the field of personal growth and development, Patricia Durovy. The subject that morning was "How to Be Happy." The common element she noted in people who feel consistently alive and joyous in life is a sense of purpose. May Fraydas, in Chapter 2, discusses the importance of knowing what you like, understanding what others will pay for, and then integrating the two. Perhaps it's even more useful to begin with the even broader dimension that these actualizers share: a sense of purpose.

What I am getting at is that you ask yourself: "What is my purpose for being on Planet Earth?" Don't run away from it, don't close the book, and don't be scared. Quietly think about it and don't feel bad if it doesn't come. Most people live their whole lives without asking this question and therefore never have an answer. Those confronted with this question often run away without discerning any inkling of their purpose.

On that radio program, Patricia offered a tool to help listeners determine what their purpose is if they can't label it. She suggested you think of your purpose as a highway. Throughout your life until now, you have zigzagged across that highway. There have been moments, when you crossed the highway, when you felt a sense of harmony, aliveness, and self-love, a sense that everything was clicking. Think about what you were doing at those moments: Were you coaching a Little League team; were you helping a friend with a problem; were you playing your violin; were you acting in a play—what was it? It's happened to you numerous times. That highway is there for all of us.

It may be helpful to give examples of other peoples' purposes. Patricia's purpose is to be at one with the universe, to be in harmony with people and things around her. For others, it is to explore and discover; for others, to be helpful; for others, to create things that didn't exist before; and for some, to love. For everyone, a purpose is something that can't be extinguished, because it's not the same as a goal. It's not something you achieve and then it's over. It's a way of being.

If you're still having trouble determining your purpose, try this. Think about what you would like to see written on your tombstone. "Here lies_____, who_____." What do you want said about you when you're gone? What words would make you feel warm, make your spine tingle, make you feel very good about yourself?

Knowing yourself will help you score well in an interview. As an interviewer, when I talk to someone I feel is answering questions the way they think they "should," I'm turned off. If they're answering with what is truly authentic, and they're integrated, I'm turned on. Knowing yourself helps you to become a desirable candidate, but perhaps more important, is that it helps you head onto the right path for your career. The exercises I suggest are exercises in self-understanding and self-awareness.

In the Fifties and Sixties and most of the Seventies, you could stay on a moving sidewalk. You could go to grammar school, high school, college, and then down the hall to the employment office. Bachelor degree in hand, you got a job with a corporation that would train you and show you the next sidewalk. You had every opportunity to remain out of touch with your inner self. You didn't have to explore—you could get by and move along. Today, that's no longer the case. A liberal arts degree *alone* won't get you much of a career without your personal input, that is, without exploring yourself to see what you want and what you have to offer the world. If you manage to avoid these introspective questions, you will skip through your career life, skimming the surface, doing your job, and looking forward to weekends and getting home every night so that you can start to have fun. If you have the courage and the will to look inside yourself, learn more of who you are and what you want, and then direct that knowledge outward in your career, those forty or fifty or more hours a week you spend working will become a reflection of your best self. Most days you will feel alive and joyful getting out of bed.

Assuming you are able to approximate if not identify your life purpose, the next step is to use it as a springboard to brainstorm careers consistent with your purpose.

If this isn't working for you, but you do have an identifiable direction and purpose, the following may help you. I have compiled a list of numerous careers that may fit your liberal arts background. Even if the careers mentioned aren't right on target, they may spark a career idea that is perfect for you. The list is compiled from *Work in the Twenty-First Century* (1984) by the American Society for Personnel Administration; *The Occupational Outlook Handbook* (1984–85 edition) by the Bureau of Labor Statistics of the U.S. Department of Labor; *The Encyclopedia of Careers and Vocational Guidance*, Volume 2, *Careers and Occupation* (1978) by William E. Hopke; *Occupations Handbook* by the Wisconsin Career Information System; and some of my own ideas.

I suggest you grab a pencil as you read this list. Check off any careers that feel good or seem interesting. After you finish reviewing it, return to the checked careers and ask yourself if they're consistent with the purpose you have defined as well as with who you are now, what you enjoy, and what skills and abilities you have to offer the world. While it is hard work, I hope this search is an energizing and joyful process which leads you to a career that adds great richness to your life.

Actor/Actress	Affirmative Action Officer
Adult Education School Owner	Agronomist
Adult Education Teacher	Alcohol and Drug Abuse Counselor
Advertising Account Executive	Animal Shelter Director
Advertising Copywriter	Animal Specialist
Advertising Manager	Announcer
Advertising Sales	Anthropologist

Antique Dealer
Archivist
Art Director
Art Therapist
Artist
Arts Administrator
Auctioneer
Author
Bank Officer
Bank Teller
Bed and Breakfast Host
Bicycle Repairer
Bicycle Trip Coordinator
Biofeedback Therapist
Budget Consultant
Buyer
Cable TV Sales
Career Counselor
Caterer
Child Advocate
Club Manager
College Placement Officer
Commercial Artist
Communications Specialist
Community College Teacher
Complaints Manager
Composer
Computer Sales
Consultant
Consultant on Giving Speeches
Copy Writer
Corrections Officer
Curator
Customer Service Representative
Day Care Center Owner
Decorator
Designer
Detective
Disc Jockey
Discussion Group Leader

Display Person
Divorce Mediator
Ecologist
Economist
Editor
Editorial Writer
Elected Official
Employee Relocation Services
   Director
Entertainer
Entertainment Manager
Environmentalist
Equal Opportunity Worker
Ethicist
Ethnicist
Exercise Technician
Exterminator
Family Mediator
Farm Manager
Fashion Designer
Financial Manager
Financial Planner
Firefighter
Fish & Game Warden
Fish & Wildlife Technician
Florist
Forester
Fund Raiser
Furniture Refinisher
Furniture Reupholsterer
Government Official
Groundskeeper
Guidance Counselor
Guide
Health Aide
Health Food Salesperson
Health Spa Exercise Leader
Helping Professional
Horticulturist
Hospital Administrator

Hotel/Restaurant Manager
Hotline Counselor
Human Resources Director
Human Services Expert
Illustrator
Image Consultant
Information Broker
Information Coordinator
Information Scientist
Insurance Examiner
Insurance Salesperson
International Salesperson
Interpreter
Job Service Specialist
Journalist
Law Enforcement Official
Legal Assistant
Librarian
Loan Officer
Management Analyst
Management Trainee
Market Research Analyst
Masseur/Masseuse
Matchmaker
Medical Records Administrator
Membership Organization
   Manager
Model
Museum Manager
Musician
Natural Resources Administrator
New Product Manager
News Editor
News Photographer
Newsletter Editor
Non-profit Agency Manager
Oceanographer
Office Green Plant Consultant
Ombudsman
Paralegal

Park Ranger
Parole Officer
Peace Corps Volunteer
Personnel Interviewer
Personnel Manager
Pharmaceutical Sales
Phobia Therapist
Plant and Pet Service
Preschool Teacher
Production Manager
Professional Lunch/Dinner
   Speaker
Proofreader
Public Health Director
Public Relations Manager
Publicity Writer
Publisher
Purchasing Agent
Purchasing Manager
Quality Control Technician
Realtor
Recreation Director
Recreation Specialist
Reporter
Research Analyst
Retail Manager
Salesperson
Secretarial & Office Support Service
Seminar Leader
Sex Therapist
Singer
Small Business Owner
Special Interest Newsletter Owner
Sportscaster
Stockbroker
Strategic Planner
Street Vendor
Stress Reduction Counselor
Talk Show Host
Teacher

Technical Writer
Telecommunications Marketer
Telephone Answering Service
    Owner
Tour Guide
Trade Association Manager
Training Officer
Translator
Travel Agent

Tutor
TV & Radio Producer
Underwriter
Urban Planner
Veterinary Aide
Videodating Service Coordinator
Vocational Rehabilitation
    Counselor
Writer for Magazines